NOTED JEWISH PEOPLE OF THE WORLD ON STAMPS

A COLLECTION OF STAMPS ISSUED BY OVER 95 COUNTRIES IN THE WORLD

By MARVIN A. BELECK

Fort Worth, Texas

DEDICATION

This book, "Noted Jewish People of the World On Stamps", is dedicated to my wife, Ava, and 3 children, Sabrina Beleck, Tamara Garsek, and Max Beleck. They have seen me work tirelessly over the past years to complete this collection, transforming it into a book, waiting for stamps to arrive from collectors and dealers all over the world, and meticulously inserting them onto pages, and also spending many hours of research at libraries. I love them dearly for allowing me to give up family time to complete this passion. Thank you!

NOTED JEWISH PEOPLE OF THE WORLD ON STAMPS

A COLLECTION OF STAMPS ISSUED BY OVER 95 COUNTRIES IN THE WORLD

By MARVIN A. BELECK
FT. WORTH, TEXAS

Marvin A. Beleck was born in Greenville, Texas in 1945 and raised in Tyler, Texas, where he attended public schools.

After graduation, he enlisted and served in the US Navy as a dental technician. He then returned to Texas, enrolled in college, and graduated from North Texas State University with a BBA in Business Management (1971). In 1973, Marvin opened a retail mattress store, Factory Mattress Outlet, which successfully operated for 43 years in Dallas and Fort Worth, Texas.

1973 was an exciting year for Marvin, as he not only started his career as a business owner, he also married Ava Fleischmann, and the two of them have three children, all whom graduated from the University of Texas, and two young grandchildren who are their pride and joy.

Marvin continuously supports his community, serving on multiple Boards and is a past President of Congregation Ahavath Sholom, their Men's Club, the Isadore Garsek B'nai B'rith Chapter of Tarrant County, and also the Jewish Education Agency. He has received multiple awards for recognition of his service; namely B'nai B'rith Jewish Person of the Year (2014), and the Congregation Ahavath Sholom President's Award (2015).

Marvin remains young at heart whilst he continues to enjoy his childhood passions of producing Jewish themed mosaics and collecting stamps from the United States, United Nations, Israel, Russia, and multiple worldwide countries.

Noted Jewish People of the World on Stamps

By Marvin A. Beleck

My passion since childhood has been stamp collecting. This special project of stamps includes over 1300 stamps honoring Jewish people of great notoriety from over 95 countries in 37 categories. This book has been a labor of love for the past ten years.

The inspiration for this book came when I received a stamp collection from a fellow philatelic collector, Mr. Klaus Driessen (Arlington, Texas). He had inherited the original collection, "Jews on Stamps" which was assembled and completed in 1971 by Mr. Walter Schiff (a very close friend of Mr. Driessen). Mr. Schiff's original collection received honors of recognition by the Philadelphia Stamp Society and other stamp organizations. My collection overlaps multiple heroes in his collection and expands the noted fields. The main cutoff date of stamp issues was 2010, though a few stamps I included were issued since that time.

The stamps may honor a person, anniversary of their death, a work of art, a historical contribution, their invention, or a simple recognition of that person. Also included are stamps with Jewish symbols, relics, Synagogues, and Israeli landscapes. Each stamp is classified by the name of the person or an item on the stamp, dates of birth and death (if known), field of knowledge, hero classification, the country issuing the stamp, and the SCOTT Identification Number or a MICHEL Identification Number. Some of these noted people have dual specialties of their works. These I have listed in the most appropriate classification. Some examples include classifications of Einstein, Leonard Bernstein, George Gershwin, or Jack Benny. Many heroes are Nobel Prize winners in their field of study and dedication. There are also Biblical themes, with sheets of stamps as evidenced in the stamps title. Such sheets of stamps include "Parting of the Red Sea by Moses", "Jonah and the Whale",
"Daniel and the Lion", and "David and Goliath". The collection also includes stamps of special interest such as a city, buildings designed by Jewish architects, symbols related to Judaism, Holocaust or Concentration Camp themes, statues, friends and supporters of the Jewish people during and after wars, or a country jointly issuing a stamp with Israel.

This is not intended to be a comprehensive collection of all issued stamps, so I tried to represent as many as possible. It remains important for me to share, with pride, this collection of original stamps in my collection. Most are in mint and unused condition without photo substitutions.

I hope you enjoy viewing my collection. These beautiful postage stamps will amaze you at the remarkable achievements, inventions, discoveries, music, art, writings, and science wonders these noted Jewish people have experienced.

Please note: *This assembly of stamps is for viewing, and not a historical collection of biographies. Complete biographical information may be found online or in print for all figures noted in this book. I have tried to be accurate in my representations but there may be some discrepencies. For my collection, a person is Jewish by birth or was considered to be Jewish by having a parent, grandparent, or great-grandparent who was Jewish or with one or both parents who were Jewish or of Jewish heritage.*

NOTED JEWISH PEOPLE OF THE WORLD ON STAMPS

Table of Contents

Introduction by Marvin Beleck

ACTORS, ENTERTAINERS

ACTORS & ENTERTAINERS

NAME: Bud Abbott
DATES LIVED: 1895-1974
NOTED FOR: Comedian, Actor
Producer CLASSIFICATION: Actor
SCOTT#: United States 2566

NAME: Jack Benny
DATES LIVED: 1894-1979
NOTED FOR: Comedian
CLASSIFICATION: Actor
SCOTT #: United States 2564

NAME: Fanny Brice
DATES LIVED: 1891-1951
NOTED FOR: Comedian, Singer
CLASSIFICATION: Actor
SCOTT #: United States 2565

NAME: Jack Benny
DATES LIVED: 1894-1979
NOTED FOR: Comedian
CLASSIFICATION: Actor
SCOTT #: Grenada 2084

NAME: Sarah Bernhardt
DATES LIVED: 1844-1923
NOTED FOR: French Stage Actress
CLASSIFICATION: Actor
SCOTT #: France B191

NAME: Nissim Aloni
DATES LIVED: 1926-1988
NOTED FOR: Theatre
CLASSIFICATION: Actor
SCOTT #: Israel 1627

NAME: Joe E. Brown
DATES LIVED: 1892-1973
NOTED FOR: Vaudville Singer, Actor
CLASSIFICATION: Actor
SCOTT #: Grenada 2087

NAME: Theda Bara
DATES LIVED: 1885-1955
NOTED FOR: Movie Star - Silent Screen
CLASSIFICATION: Actor
SCOTT #: United States 2827

NAME: Werner Otto Klemperer
DATES LIVED: 1920-2000
NOTED FOR: Comedian, Actor
CLASSIFICATION: Actor
SCOTT #: Germany 9N502

ACTORS & ENTERTAINERS

NAME: Douglas Fairbanks
DATES LIVED: 1883-1939
NOTED FOR: Actor
CLASSIFICATION: Actor
SCOTT #: United States 2088

NAME: Judy Garland
DATES LIVED: 1922-1969
NOTED FOR: American Actress, Singer
CLASSIFICATION: Actor
SCOTT #: Antigua 1043

NAME: Moshe Halevy
DATES LIVED: 1895-1974
NOTED FOR: Theatre
CLASSIFICATION: Actor
SCOTT #: Israel 1625

NAME: Al Josen
DATES LIVED: 1886-1950
NOTED FOR: Singer, Theater, Movies
CLASSIFICATION: Actor
SCOTT #: Tanzania 1480

NAME: Rock Hudson
DATES LIVED: 1925-1985
NOTED FOR: (Ray Harold Scherer) American
Film & TV Star
CLASSIFICATION: Actor
SCOTT #: Antigua 1045

NAME: Danny Kaye
DATES LIVED: 1913-1987
NOTED FOR: Singer, Actor
CLASSIFICATION: Actor
SCOTT #: Grenada 2089

NAME: Al Josen
DATES LIVED: 1886-1950
NOTED FOR: Singer, Theater, Movies
CLASSIFICATION: Actor
SCOTT #: United States 2849

NAME: Danny Kaye
DATES LIVED: 1913-1987
NOTED FOR: Singer, Actor
CLASSIFICATION: Actor
SCOTT #: Gambia 774

ACTORS & ENTERTAINERS

NAME: Marilyn Monroe
DATES LIVED: 1926-1962
NOTED FOR: Actress
CLASSIFICATION: Actor
SCOTT #: United States 2967

NAME: Marilyn Monroe
DATES LIVED: 1926-1962
NOTED FOR: Actress
CLASSIFICATION: Actor
SCOTT #: Antigua 1041

NAME: Joseph Millo
DATES LIVED: 1916-1997
NOTED FOR: Theatre
CLASSIFICATION: Actor
SCOTT #: Israel 1624

Golden Bear award
Berlin Film Festival, 1974
Ours d'or
Festival du film de Berlin, 1974

NAME: Groucho Marx
DATES LIVED: 1890-1977
NOTED FOR: Comedian, Actor
CLASSIFICATION: Actor
SCOTT #: Gambia 776

NAME: Chico Marx
DATES LIVED: 1887-1961
NOTED FOR: Comedian, Actor, Movies
CLASSIFICATION: Actor
SCOTT #: Gambia 776

NAME: Gummo Marx
DATES LIVED: 1893-1977
NOTED FOR: Comedian, Actor, Movies
CLASSIFICATION: Actor
SCOTT #: Gambia 776

NAME: Harpo Marx
DATES LIVED: 1888-1964
NOTED FOR: Comedian, Actor, Movies
CLASSIFICATION: Actor
SCOTT #: Gambia 776

NAME: Duddy Kravitz
DATES LIVED: 1959-date
NOTED FOR: Movie of Jewish Life in Canada
CLASSIFICATION: Actor
SCOTT #: Canada 1616b

ACTORS & ENTERTAINERS

NAME: Hannah Rovina
DATES LIVED: 1889-1980
NOTED FOR: Actress
CLASSIFICATION: Actor
SCOTT #: Israel 1102

NAME: Ethel Rosenberg
DATES LIVED: 1915-1953
NOTED FOR: Actress, Singer, Executed for Conspiracy
CLASSIFICATION: Actor
SCOTT #: Cuba C313

NAME: Simone Signoret
DATES LIVED: 1921-1985
NOTED FOR: French Theatre, Movies
CLASSIFICATION: Actor
SCOTT #: France B685

NAME: Leonard Nimoy Nimon(Star Trek)
DATES LIVED: 1931-date
NOTED FOR: American Actor
CLASSIFICATION: Actor
SCOTT #: St. Vincent 2545a

NAME: Shai Ophir
DATES LIVED: 1928-1987
NOTED FOR: Israel Theatre Actor
CLASSIFICATION: Actor
SCOTT #: Israel 1626

NAME: Phil Silvers
DATES LIVED: 1911-1985
NOTED FOR: American Actor, Comedian
CLASSIFICATION: Actor
SCOTT #: Grenada 2088

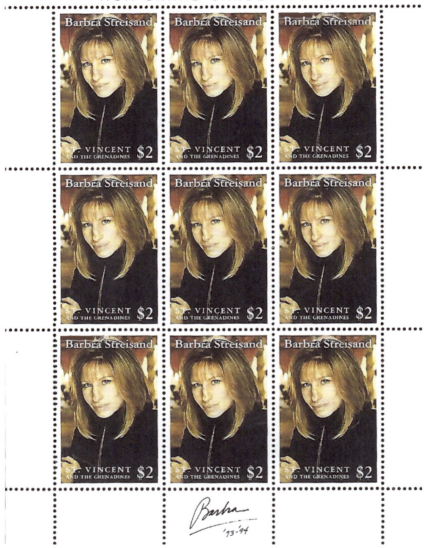

NAME: Barbara Streisand
DATES LIVED: 1942-date
NOTED FOR: American Singer, Actress, Director
CLASSIFICATION: Actor
SCOTT #: St. Vincent (9) 2011 Sheet

ACTORS & ENTERTAINERS

NAME: Eddie Cantor
DATES LIVED: 1892-1964
NOTED FOR: Comedian, Singer, Actor
CLASSIFICATION: Actor
SCOTT #: Grenada 2552

NAME: Peter Sellers
DATES LIVED: 1925-1980
NOTED FOR: British Theatre, Movies
CLASSIFICATION: Actor
SCOTT #: Dominica 1845

NAME: Gertrude Berg
DATES LIVED: 1899-1966
NOTED FOR: Radio & Television Actress
CLASSIFICATION: Actor
SCOTT #: Grenada 2551

NAME: Groucho Marx
DATES LIVED: 1890-1977
NOTED FOR: Comedian, Actor
CLASSIFICATION: Actor
SCOTT #: Grenada 2553

NAME: Sarah Bernhardt
DATES LIVED: 1844-1923
NOTED FOR: French Stage Actress
CLASSIFICATION: Actor
SCOTT #: Monaco 1931

ACTORS & ENTERTAINERS

NAME: Larry, Curly, Moe Three Stooges
DATES LIVED:
NOTED FOR: Comedy Film Actors - 1999 sheet
CLASSIFICATION: Actors
MICHEL #: Senegal 1887 (9) Sheet

NAME: Joe E. Brown
DATES LIVED: 1892-1973
NOTED FOR: Vaudville Singer, Actor
CLASSIFICATION: Actor
SCOTT #: Gambia 1993

ACTORS & ENTERTAINERS

NAME: Larry, Curly, Moe Three Stooges
DATES LIVED:
NOTED FOR: Comedy Film Actors - 1999 sheets
CLASSIFICATION: Actors
SCOTT #: Senegal (2) 1433-34 M/S

NAME: Larry Fine
DATES LIVED: 1902-1975
NOTED FOR: Movie and Television Actor- Three Stooges
CLASSIFICATION: Actor
SCOTT #: Senegal 1433-34

NAME: Moe Howard
DATES LIVED: 1897-1975
NOTED FOR: Movie and Television Actor- Three Stooges
CLASSIFICATION: Actor
SCOTT #: Senegal 1433-34

NAME: Shrimp Howard
DATES LIVED: 1895-1955
NOTED FOR: Movie and Television Actor- Three Stooges
CLASSIFICATION: Actor
SCOTT #: Senegal 1433-34

ACTORS & ENTERTAINERS

NAME: Groucho Marx
DATES LIVED: 1890-1977
NOTED FOR: Comedian, Actor
CLASSIFICATION: Actor
SCOTT #: Ghana 1942

NAME: Jerry Lewis
DATES LIVED: 1926-date
NOTED FOR: American Comedian, Actor, Writer
CLASSIFICATION: Actor
SCOTT #: Ghana 1909

NAME: Zero Mostel
DATES LIVED: 1915-1977
NOTED FOR: American Film & Stage Actor
CLASSIFICATION: Actor
SCOTT #: Antigua & Barbuda 2037c

ACTORS & ENTERTAINERS

NAME: George Burns
DATES LIVED: 1896-1996
NOTED FOR: American Actor, Comedian, Writer
CLASSIFICATION: Actor
SCOTT #: Grenada 2554

NAME: Gracie Allen
DATES LIVED: 1895-1964
NOTED FOR: American Comedian
CLASSIFICATION: Actor
SCOTT #: Grenada 2554

NAME: Bud Abbott
DATES LIVED: 1895-1974
NOTED FOR: Comedian, Actor Producer
CLASSIFICATION: Actor
SCOTT #: Gambia 1348d

NAME: Marilyn Monroe
DATES LIVED: 1926-1962
NOTED FOR: Actress
CLASSIFICATION: Actor
SCOTT #: Marshall Islands (12) 592 Sheet

KIRK DOUGLAS

Grenada/Carriacou & Petite Martinique $1.50
Grenada/Carriacou & Petite Martinique $1.50
Grenada/Carriacou & Petite Martinique $1.50
Grenada/Carriacou & Petite Martinique $1.50
Grenada/Carriacou & Petite Martinique $1.50
Grenada/Carriacou & Petite Martinique $1.50

Kirk Douglas has been one of the world's most famous entertainers of the 20th century, having starred in over eighty motion pictures spanning more than fifty years. He is the recipient of numerous entertainment awards including the Golden Globe, Cecil B. DeMille Award, Academy Award (for lifetime achievement) and the Presidential Medal of Freedom. As an Actor and sometimes Producer, Douglas has starred in some of the most popular films of all time including Champion, The Bad and the Beautiful, Lust For Life and Spartacus. He has also penned two novels and a best selling autobiography.

NAME: Kirk Douglas
DATES LIVED: 1916-date
NOTED FOR: Actor, Filmstar
CLASSIFICATION: Actor
SCOTT #: Grenada (6)2136-41 `Sheet

ACTORS & ENTERTAINERS

NAME: Dinah Shore
DATES LIVED: 1916-1994
NOTED FOR: Singer, Actress
CLASSIFICATION: Actors, Entertainers
SCOTT #: Antigua & Barbuda 2014

NAME: Hedy Lamaar
DATES LIVED: 1914-2000
NOTED FOR: Austrian American Hollywood
Superstar
CLASSIFICATION: Actors, Entertainers
SCOTT #: Austria 2296

NAME: Joseph Schmidt
DATES LIVED: 1904-1942
NOTED FOR: Austrian- Hungarian Opera Singer and
Cantor, Tenor
CLASSIFICATION: Actors, Entertainers
SCOTT #: Germany 2274

NAME: Theda Bara
DATES LIVED: 1885-1955
NOTED FOR: Movie Star, Silent Movies
CLASSIFICATION: Actors, Entertainers
SCOTT #: Fujeira Mi 1140A

NAME: Billy Wilder
DATES LIVED: 1906-2002
NOTED FOR: Austrian born Samuel Wilder, Actor,
Producer, Filmmaker
CLASSIFICATION: Actors, Entertainers
SCOTT #: United States 4670

NAME: Dinah Shore
DATES LIVED: 1916-1994
NOTED FOR: Singer, Actress
CLASSIFICATION: Actors, Entertainers
SCOTT #: United States 4414-i

ACTORS & ENTERTAINERS

NAME: George Burns
DATES LIVED: 1896-1996
NOTED FOR: American Actor
CLASSIFICATION: Actors, Entertainers
SCOTT #: United States 4414P

NAME: Gracie Allen
DATES LIVED: 1895-1964
NOTED FOR: American Actor,
teamed with George Burns
CLASSIFICATION: Actors, Entertainers
SCOTT #: United States 4414P

NAME: Groucho Marx
DATES LIVED: 1890-1977
NOTED FOR: Comedian, Actor, Tv show Host
CLASSIFICATION: Actors, Entertainers
SCOTT #: United States 4414H

NAME: Lauren Bacall
DATES LIVED: 1924-2014
NOTED FOR: (Betty Joan Perske) - Actress, Singer,

Movie Star
CLASSIFICATION: Actors, Entertainers
SCOTT #: Senegal 1425F

NAME: Katherine Hepburn
DATES LIVED: 1907-2003
NOTED FOR: American Actress- of Jewish descent
Sewell Hepbron
CLASSIFICATION: Actors, Entertainers
SCOTT #: Senegal 1425B

NAME: Victor Borge
DATES LIVED: 1909-2000
NOTED FOR: born Borge Rosenbaum,
Entertainer, Pianist
CLASSIFICATION: Actors,
Entertainers
SCOTT #: Denmark 1394

ACTORS & ENTERTAINERS

NAME: Robbie Robertson
DATES LIVED: 1943-present
NOTED FOR: Canadian musician, Jewish Father,
Singer, Songwriter
CLASSIFICATION: Actors, Entertainers
SCOTT #: Canada 2482B

NAME: Michel Berger
DATES LIVED: 1947-1992
NOTED FOR: Singer
CLASSIFICATION: Musicians
SCOTT #: France 2823

NAME: Daniel Radcliffe
DATES LIVED: 1989-present
NOTED FOR: English Actor, Harry Potter
CLASSIFICATION: Actors, Entertainers
SCOTT #: France 3303

ACTORS & ENTERTAINERS

NAME: Leila Mourad
DATES LIVED: 1918-1965
NOTED FOR: Father of Jewish descent, Egyptian
Singer-Actress
CLASSIFICATION: Actors, Singers
SCOTT #: Egypt 1731

NAME: Serge (Lucien) Gainsbourg (Goldberg)
DATES LIVED: 1928-1991
NOTED FOR: French Singer, pianist, song writer
CLASSIFICATION: Composers , Musicians
SCOTT #: France 2821

NAME: Barbara (Monique) Serf
DATES LIVED: 1930-1997
NOTED FOR: Singer
CLASSIFICATION: Musicians
SCOTT #: France 2824

NAME: Roy Rene
DATES LIVED: 1891-1954
NOTED FOR: Australian comedian- born Harry van
der Sluys
CLASSIFICATION: Comedians
SCOTT #: Australia 1142

NAME: Grethe Weiser
DATES LIVED: 1903-1970
NOTED FOR: Married Jewish man- Financed
Husband- Actress
CLASSIFICATION: Actors, Entertainers
SCOTT #: Germany 1726

NAME: Phil Silvers
DATES LIVED: 1911-1985
NOTED FOR: American Actor, Comedian
CLASSIFICATION: Actors, Entertainers
SCOTT #: United States 4414L

ACTORS & ENTERTAINERS

NAME: Peter Ustinov
DATES LIVED: 1921-2004
NOTED FOR: English Actor, Writer, Film Maker, Dir.
CLASSIFICATION: Actors, Entertainers
SCOTT #: Dominica 1845i

NAME: Olivia Newton-John
DATES LIVED: 1948-present
NOTED FOR: English-Austrailian singer, writer,
grandfather Jewish
CLASSIFICATION: Actors, Entertainers
SCOTT #: Australia B6

NAME: Sammy Davis, Jr.
DATES LIVED: 1925-1990
NOTED FOR: Singer, Converted to Judiasm,
Entertainer, Dancer
CLASSIFICATION: Actors, Entertainers
SCOTT #: Malagasy Republic 1055

NAME: Michael Douglas
DATES LIVED: 1944-present
NOTED FOR: UN Messenger of Peace, movie star,
actor, producer
CLASSIFICATION: Statesmen
SCOTT #: Sierra Leone 2846A-B

NAME: Therese Giehse
DATES LIVED: 1898-1975
NOTED FOR: German Actress, born Therese Gift
CLASSIFICATION: Actors, Entertainers
SCOTT #: Germany 1484

ACTORS & ENTERTAINERS

NAME: Lorne Greene
DATES LIVED: 1915-1987
NOTED FOR: Canadian Star of Bonanza, Actor
CLASSIFICATION: Actors, Entertainers
SCOTT #: Canada 2153A-D

NAME: Cyndi Lauper
DATES LIVED: 1953-present
NOTED FOR: American Singer, Pop Culture Music
CLASSIFICATION: Actors, Entertainers
SCOTT #: Mali Mi1452

NAME: Carly Simon
DATES LIVED: 1945-present
NOTED FOR: Singer, songwriter, author, musician
CLASSIFICATION: Musicians
SCOTT #: Mali MI145

ACTORS & ENTERTAINERS

NAME: Melvyn Douglas
DATES LIVED: 1901-1981
NOTED FOR: father Jewish, American Actor
CLASSIFICATION: Actors, Entertainers
SCOTT #: Senegal 1425C

NAME: Ed (Isiah Edwin) Wynn (Leopold)
DATES LIVED: 1886-1966
NOTED FOR: Actor, Comedian, Radio Show Host
CLASSIFICATION: Actors, Entertainers
SCOTT #: Grenada Grenadines 1842

NAME: Paul Newman
DATES LIVED: 1925-2008
NOTED FOR: Famous Actor, Friend of Jews, Father

Jewish, Philanthropist, Director

CLASSIFICATION: Actors, Entertainers
SCOTT #: St. Thomas & Prince Islands 1956

NAME: Winona Ryder
DATES LIVED: 1971-present
NOTED FOR: American Singer, Actress
CLASSIFICATION: Actors, Entertainers
SCOTT #: Abkhasia 1999 Illegal Sheet

NAME: Edward G. (Emanuel) Robinson (Goldenberg)
DATES LIVED: 1893-1973
NOTED FOR: Romanian born Actor, Performed in over
100 movies
CLASSIFICATION: Actors, Entertainers
SCOTT #: United States 3446

NAME: Bert Lahr
DATES LIVED: 1895-1967
NOTED FOR: American actor, Played the Tin Man in
Wizard of Oz
CLASSIFICATION: Actors, Entertainers
SCOTT #: Mali 728

ARTISTS, PAINTERS

ARTISTS & PAINTERS

NAME: Yaacov Agam
DATES LIVED: 1928-date
NOTED FOR: Painter, Artist, Designer
"Independence Day"
CLASSIFICATION: Artist, Painter
SCOTT #: Israel 838

NAME: Marc Chagall
DATES LIVED: 1887-1985
NOTED FOR: Russian Painter
CLASSIFICATION: Artist, Painter
SCOTT #: Monaco 1599

NAME: Chaim Nachman Bialik
DATES LIVED: 1873-1934
NOTED FOR: Artist
CLASSIFICATION: Artist, Painter
SCOTT #: Israel 155

NAME: Mordechai Ardon
DATES LIVED: 1896-1992
NOTED FOR: Abstractionist, Painter - "Jerusalem
Painting"
CLASSIFICATION: Artist, Painter
SCOTT #: Israel 773

NAME: Marc Chagall
DATES LIVED: 1887-1985
NOTED FOR: Russian Painter
CLASSIFICATION: Artist, Painter
SCOTT #: Israel 399

NAME: Jankel Adler
DATES LIVED: 1895-1949
NOTED FOR: Printmaker, Painter -"The Purim
Players"
CLASSIFICATION: Artist, Painter
SCOTT #: Israel 568

ARTISTS & PAINTERS

NAME: Haim Glicksberg
DATES LIVED: 1904-1970
NOTED FOR: Painter, Artist - "Street In Jerusalem"
CLASSIFICATION: Artist, Painter
SCOTT #: Israel 682

NAME: James Ensor
DATES LIVED: 1860-1949
NOTED FOR: Belgium Painter
CLASSIFICATION: Artist, Painter
SCOTT #: Israel 1365a

NAME: Aharon Kahana
DATES LIVED: 1905-1967
NOTED FOR: Sculptor, Painter, Artist -
"Resurrection
CLASSIFICATION: Artist, Painter
SCOTT #: Israel 483

NAME: Maurycy Gottlieb
DATES LIVED: 1856-1879
NOTED FOR: Printmaker, Painter - "Yom Kippur"
CLASSIFICATION: Artist, Painter
SCOTT #: Israel 569

ARTISTS & PAINTERS

NAME: Michaelangelo Buonarroti Isaiah
DATES LIVED: 1475-1564
NOTED FOR: Artist
CLASSIFICATION: Artist, Painter
SCOTT #: Vatican City 388

NAME: Moshe Kisling
DATES LIVED: 1891-1953
NOTED FOR: Painter - "Lady In Blue"
CLASSIFICATION: Artist, Painter
SCOTT #: Israel 537

NAME: Leopold Krakauer
DATES LIVED: 1890-1954
NOTED FOR: Painter, Artist - "Thistles"
CLASSIFICATION: Artist, Painter
SCOTT #: Israel 683

NAME: Moshe Kisling
DATES LIVED: 1891-1953
NOTED FOR: Landscape Artist
CLASSIFICATION: Artist, Painter
SCOTT #: Bulgaria 3525

NAME: Yosef Kukovski
DATES LIVED: 1902-1969
NOTED FOR: Russian Artist, Painter - "The Last Way"
CLASSIFICATION: Artist, Painter
SCOTT #: Israel 843

NAME: Lasar Segal
DATES LIVED: 1891-1957
NOTED FOR: Brazilian Painter
CLASSIFICATION: Artist, Painter
SCOTT #: Brazil 2339

NAME: Aryeh Lubin
DATES LIVED: 1897-1980
NOTED FOR: Painter, Artist -Tel Aviv Landscape
CLASSIFICATION: Artist, Painter
SCOTT #: Israel 815

NAME: Mordechai Levanon
DATES LIVED: 1901-1968
NOTED FOR: Painter, Artist - "An Alley In Zefat"
CLASSIFICATION: Artist, Painter
SCOTT #: Israel 684

ARTISTS & PAINTERS

NAME: Amedeo Modigeliani
DATES LIVED: 1884-1920
NOTED FOR: Italian Economist, Artist
CLASSIFICATION: Artist, Painter
SCOTT #: France 1693

NAME: Nicholus Poussin Moses
DATES LIVED: 1594-1665
NOTED FOR: French Painter
CLASSIFICATION: Artist, Painter
SCOTT #: France 2435

NAME: Chana Orloff
DATES LIVED: 1888-1968
NOTED FOR: Sculptor, Painter - "Mother & Child"
CLASSIFICATION: Artist, Painter
SCOTT #: Israel 538

NAME: Moritz D. Oppenheim
DATES LIVED: 1800-1882
NOTED FOR: Abstractionist, Painter - "Hannukah"
CLASSIFICATION: Artist, Painter
SCOTT #: Israel 567

NAME: Boris Pasternak
DATES LIVED: 1890-1960
NOTED FOR: Russian Artist, Painter
CLASSIFICATION: Artist, Painter
SCOTT #: Russia 5939

NAME: Abel Pann
DATES LIVED: 1883-1963
NOTED FOR: Artist - "Young Girl"
CLASSIFICATION: Artist, Painter
SCOTT #: Israel 480

NAME: Israel Paldi
DATES LIVED: 1892-1979
NOTED FOR: Israeli Artist, Painter
CLASSIFICATION: Artist, Painter
SCOTT #: Israel 817

NAME: Max Liebermann
DATES LIVED: 1847-1935
NOTED FOR: German Jewish Painter
CLASSIFICATION: Artist
SCOTT #: Germany 431

ARTISTS & PAINTERS

NAME: Mordechai Ardon
DATES LIVED: 1896-1992
NOTED FOR: Stained Glass Artist
CLASSIFICATION: Artist, Painter
SCOTT #: Israel (2) 1041 S/S

NAME: Juliusz Kossak
DATES LIVED: 1824-1899
NOTED FOR: Polish Artist
CLASSIFICATION: Artist, Painter
SCOTT #: Israel 1772

NAME: Berek Joselewicz
DATES LIVED: 1764-1809
NOTED FOR: Colonel of the Polish Army
CLASSIFICATION: Military
SCOTT #: Israel 1772 S/S

ARTISTS & PAINTERS

NAME: Max Liebermann
DATES LIVED: 1847-1935
NOTED FOR: German Jewish Painter
CLASSIFICATION: Artist
SCOTT #: Germany 2970

NAME: Omer Hillel
DATES LIVED: 1926-date
NOTED FOR: Artist
CLASSIFICATION: Artist, Painter
SCOTT #: Israel 894

NAME: David Polus
DATES LIVED: 1886-1947
NOTED FOR: Ukranian Artist, Sculptor
CLASSIFICATION: Artist, Painter
SCOTT #: Israel 863

NAME: Chana Orloff
DATES LIVED: 1888-1968
NOTED FOR: Artist
CLASSIFICATION: Artist, Painter
SCOTT #: Israel 865

NAME: Reuven Rubin
DATES LIVED: 1893-1974
NOTED FOR: Painter, Artist - "Dancers Of Meron"
CLASSIFICATION: Artist, Painter
SCOTT #: Israel 599

NAME: Abraham Melnikov
DATES LIVED: 1892-1960
NOTED FOR: Artist
CLASSIFICATION: Artist, Painter
SCOTT #: Israel 864

ARTISTS & PAINTERS

NAME: Boris Schatz
DATES LIVED: 1867-1932
NOTED FOR: Lithuanian Sculptor, Artist - "The Scribe"
CLASSIFICATION: Artist, Painter
SCOTT #: Israel 479

NAME: Chaim Soutine
DATES LIVED: 1893-1943
NOTED FOR: Painter, Artist, Expressionist - "Girl In Blue"
CLASSIFICATION: Artist, Painter
SCOTT #: Israel 539

NAME: Menachim Shemi
DATES LIVED: 1879-1951
NOTED FOR: Artist
CLASSIFICATION: Artist, Painter
SCOTT #: Israel 481

NAME: Jacob Steinhardt
DATES LIVED: 1887-1968
NOTED FOR: Woodcut Artist, Painter - "Old Jerusalem"
CLASSIFICATION: Artist, Painter
SCOTT #: Israel 482

NAME: Anna Ticho
DATES LIVED: 1894-1980
NOTED FOR: Artist of Jerusalem Hills
CLASSIFICATION: Artist, Painter
SCOTT #: Israel 771

ARTISTS & PAINTERS

NAME: Frida Kahlo
DATES LIVED: 1907-1954
NOTED FOR: German Jewish Father, Mexican
Artist, married Diego Kahlo
CLASSIFICATION: Artists, Painters
SCOTT #: Mexico 2228

NAME: Louis J. Pierard
DATES LIVED: 1886-1951
NOTED FOR: Belgian Writer, Artist, Sculptor
CLASSIFICATION: Writers
SCOTT #: Belgium 860

NAME: Lasar Segall
DATES LIVED: 1891-1957
NOTED FOR: Brazilian Painter, Artist and Birth
Centinary
CLASSIFICATION: Artists
SCOTT #: Brazil 2339

NAME: Marianne M. Nagler
DATES LIVED: 1943-present
NOTED FOR: Artist, designed Jewish themed stamp
for Denmark, 'Sabbath Candles'
CLASSIFICATION: Ariists, Painters
SCOTT #: Denmark 766

NAME: Barbu Iscovescu
DATES LIVED: 1816-1854
NOTED FOR: Painter, Revolutionary Painter
CLASSIFICATION: Artists, Painters
SCOTT #: Romania 2353

ARTISTS & PAINTERS

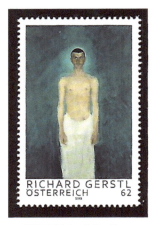

NAME: Richard Gerstl
DATES LIVED: 1883-1908
NOTED FOR: Austrian painter& draughtsman
CLASSIFICATION: Painters
SCOTT #: Austria 2453

NAME: Max Liebermann
DATES LIVED: 1847-1935
NOTED FOR: Painter
CLASSIFICATION: Artists, Painters
SCOTT #: Germany 1878

NAME: C.D. Rosenthal
DATES LIVED: 1820-1851
NOTED FOR: Romanian Painter, Sculptor
CLASSIFICATION: Artists, Painters
SCOTT #: Romania Mi1268-69

NAME: C.D. Rosenthal
DATES LIVED: 1820-1851
NOTED FOR: Romanian Painter, Sculptor
CLASSIFICATION: Artists, Painters
SCOTT #: Romania Mi 1270-71

ARTISTS & PAINTERS

NAME: Y.M. Pen
DATES LIVED:
NOTED FOR: Famous Painter, 'Old Jew Reading
Yiddish'
CLASSIFICATION: Artists
SCOTT #: Belarus 530

NAME: Frederick John (Jacob) Kiesler
DATES LIVED: 1890-1965
NOTED FOR: Austrian-American Artist,
Sculptor,designer
CLASSIFICATION: Artists, Painters
SCOTT #: Austria 2579

NAME: Felix Nussbaum
DATES LIVED: 1904-1944
NOTED FOR: German Jewish Artist, died Auschwitz
CLASSIFICATION: Artists, Painters
SCOTT #: Germany 2303

ARTISTS & PAINTERS

NAME: E. Moshe Lilien
DATES LIVED: 1874-1925
NOTED FOR: Founder- Bezalel Academy of Art,
Zionist themed art
CLASSIFICATION: Artists, Painters
SCOTT #: Israel 625-627

NAME: Odette Caly
DATES LIVED: 1914-1993
NOTED FOR: French Artist, 'La Corbeille Rose"
CLASSIFICATION: Artists, Painters
SCOTT #: France Mi 2473

NAME: Odssip Zadkine
DATES LIVED: 1890-1967
NOTED FOR: Russian Artist, Sculptor, Painter,
Lithographer
CLASSIFICATION: Artists, Painters
SCOTT #: France 2192

ARTISTS & PAINTERS

NAME: Sionah Tagger
DATES LIVED: 1892-1979
NOTED FOR: Painter, Artist - "Landscapes"
CLASSIFICATION: Artist, Painter
SCOTT #: Israel 816

NAME: Joseph Zaritsky
DATES LIVED: 1891-1985
NOTED FOR: Artist, Painter - "Jerusalem Painting"
CLASSIFICATION: Artist, Painter
SCOTT #: Israel 772

NAME: Isaak Levitan
DATES LIVED: 1860-1900
NOTED FOR: Painter
CLASSIFICATION: Artists, Painters
SCOTT #: Russia 7235

NAME: Endre Nemes
DATES LIVED: 1909-1985
NOTED FOR: Surrealist Artist, Enamels used in art
CLASSIFICATION: Artists, Painters
SCOTT #: Slovakia 255 M/S

NAME: Sophie Tauber
DATES LIVED: 1889-1943
NOTED FOR: Swiss Artist, Painter, Sculptor, Dada Art
Movement, Textile designs
CLASSIFICATION: Artists, Painters
SCOTT #: Switzerland 2425

NAME: Sophie Tauber
DATES LIVED: 1889-1943
NOTED FOR: Swiss Artist, Painter, Sculptor, Dada Art
Movement, Textile designs
CLASSIFICATION: Artists, Painters
SCOTT #: Switzerland 2426

NAME: Dominik Skutecky
DATES LIVED: 1849-1921
NOTED FOR: Painter
CLASSIFICATION: Artists, Painters
SCOTT #: Slovakia 341

NAME: Ofra Kestenbaum
DATES LIVED: -Present
NOTED FOR: Israeli Graphic Artist, Subject

on stamp by Asher Kalderon
CLASSIFICATION: Artists, Painters
SCOTT #: Maldives 633

Нестор-летописец (фрагмент статуи).
Мрамор. 1889.

Пишите индекс предприятия связи места назначения

Художник Ю. Арцименев © Федеральное управление почтовой связи при Мин. связи РФ. Издатцентр «Марка», 1993. З. 2138. МТ Гознака. Т. 250 тыс 27. 01. 93.

М.М. Антокольский 1843-1902

4 руб. РОССИЯ Rossija 1993

Куда _____

Кому _____

Индекс предприятия связи и адрес отправителя

NAME: Mark Antokololsky
DATES LIVED: 1843-1902
NOTED FOR: Russian Sculptor
CLASSIFICATION: Artists, Painters
SCOTT #: Russia 1993 Post Card

ASTRONAUTS

ASTRONAUTS

NAME: Boris Volynov
DATES LIVED: 1934-date
NOTED FOR: Soviet Space Astronaut
CLASSIFICATION: Astronaut
SCOTT #: Russia 3571 S/S

NAME: Ilan Ramon
DATES LIVED: 1954-2003
NOTED FOR: Astronaut
CLASSIFICATION: Astronaut
SCOTT #: Israel 1552

ATHLETES

ATHLETES

NAME: Mark Spitz
DATES LIVED: 1950-date
NOTED FOR: Seven Gold Medals in Swimming
CLASSIFICATION: Athlete
SCOTT #: Grenada Grenadines 1695

NAME: Mark Spitz
DATES LIVED: 1950-present
NOTED FOR: American Swimmer, Won 7 Gold Medals
CLASSIFICATION: Athletes
SCOTT #: Fujeira 1454

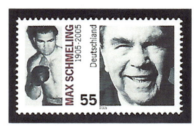

NAME: Max Schmeling
DATES LIVED: 1905-2005
NOTED FOR: German boxing World Heavyweight Champion
CLASSIFICATION: Athletes
SCOTT #: Germany 2354

NAME: Max Schmeling
DATES LIVED: 1905-2005
NOTED FOR: German boxing World Heavyweight Champion
CLASSIFICATION: Athletes
SCOTT #: Austria 1988

NAME: Hank B. Greenberg
DATES LIVED: 1911-1986
NOTED FOR: "Hammerin Hank", Hall of Fame
CLASSIFICATION: Athletes
SCOTT #: United States 4081

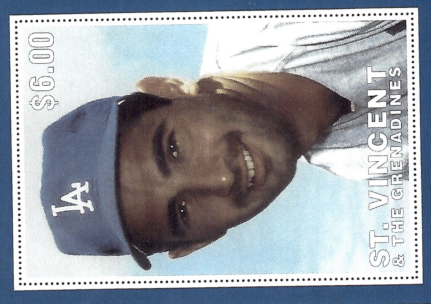

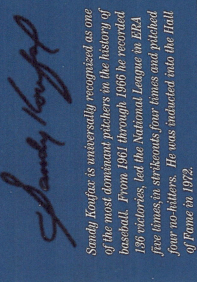

SPORTS LEGENDS

ST. VINCENT & THE GRENADINES

$6.00

Sandy Koufax is universally recognized as one of the most dominant pitchers in the history of baseball. From 1961 through 1966 he recorded 136 victories, led the National League in ERA five times, in strikeouts four times and pitched four no-hitters. He was inducted into the Hall of Fame in 1972.

2050

NAME: Sandy Koufax
DATES LIVED: 1935-present
NOTED FOR: Baseball Star Pitcher
CLASSIFICATION: Athletes
SCOTT #: St. Vincent 2356 A-D Sheet

ATHLETES

NAME: Fanny Rosenfield
DATES LIVED: 1904-1969
NOTED FOR: Canadian Athlete, Runner
CLASSIFICATION: Athlete
SCOTT #: Canada 1610

BROADCASTERS

BROADCASTERS

NAME: Walter Lippman
DATES LIVED: 1889-1974
NOTED FOR: American Political Commentator
CLASSIFICATION: Broadcasters
SCOTT #: United States 1849

BUSINESSMEN, FINANCIERS

BUSINESSMEN & FINANCIERS

NAME: Marcel Dassault
DATES LIVED: 1892-1986
NOTED FOR: French Aircraft Industrialist
CLASSIFICATION: Businessman
SCOTT #: France 2085

NAME: Donna Gracia
DATES LIVED: 1510-1569
NOTED FOR: Philanthropist
CLASSIFICATION: Financier, Businessman
SCOTT #: Israel 1097

NAME: Yehoshua Hankin
DATES LIVED: 1865-1945
NOTED FOR: Land Developer
CLASSIFICATION: Businessman
SCOTT #: Israel 1545

NAME: Leon Yehuda Recanati
DATES LIVED: 1890-1945
NOTED FOR: Financier
CLASSIFICATION: Financier, Businessman
SCOTT #: Israel 918

NAME: Akiva Aryeh Weiss
DATES LIVED: 1868-1947
NOTED FOR: Developer, Builder
CLASSIFICATION: Financier,
Businessman SCOTT #: Israel 1717

NAME: Haym Solomon
DATES LIVED: 1740-1785
NOTED FOR: Financed Continental Army
CLASSIFICATION: Financier, Businessman
SCOTT #: United States 1561

NAME: Raoul Wallenberg
DATES LIVED: 1912-1947
NOTED FOR: Swedish Businessman,Diplomant
CLASSIFICATION: Businessman
SCOTT #: Dominica 1134

NAME: David Wolffson
DATES LIVED: 1856-1914
NOTED FOR: Banker
CLASSIFICATION: Businessman
SCOTT #: Israel 888

BUSINESSMEN & FINANCIERS

NAME: Raoul Wallenberg
DATES LIVED: 1912-1947
NOTED FOR: Swedish Businessman,Diplomant
CLASSIFICATION: Businessman
SCOTT #: Israel 842

NAME: Raoul Wallenberg
DATES LIVED: 1912-1947
NOTED FOR: Swedish Businessman,Diplomant
CLASSIFICATION: Businessman
SCOTT #: Argentina 2026

NAME: Raoul Wallenberg
DATES LIVED: 1912-1947
NOTED FOR: Swedish Businessman,Diplomant
CLASSIFICATION: Businessman
SCOTT #: Sweden 1643

NAME: Raoul Wallenberg
DATES LIVED: 1912-1947
NOTED FOR: Swedish Businessman, Diplomant
CLASSIFICATION: Businessman
SCOTT #: United States 3135

NAME: Simone Weisenthal
DATES LIVED: 1908-2005
NOTED FOR: Austrian Hunter of Nazi War Criminals
CLASSIFICATION: Financier, Businessman
SCOTT #: Israel 1820

BUSINESSMEN & FINANCIERS

NAME: Santos Dumont
DATES LIVED: 1873-1932
NOTED FOR: Brazilian who Sponsored Flight
Around Eiffel Tower Aviator,
CLASSIFICATION: Financiers, Businessmen
SCOTT #: Brazil 713-14

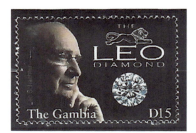

NAME: Leo Schachter
DATES LIVED: 1914-1995
NOTED FOR: NY-Israeli Diamond merchant, named
Leo Diamond
CLASSIFICATION: Financiers, Businessmen
SCOTT #: Gambia 2774

NAME: Loti Smorgon
DATES LIVED: 1919-2013
NOTED FOR: Philanthropist, Meat, steel industry
CLASSIFICATION: Financiers, Businessmen
SCOTT #: Australia 2778A

NAME: Victor Smorgon
DATES LIVED: 1913-2009
NOTED FOR: Australian Industrialist, father had
    kosher deli
CLASSIFICATION: Financiers, Businessmen
SCOTT #: Australia 2778A

NAME: Alberto (brother Aste) Bolaffi
DATES LIVED: 1874-1944
NOTED FOR: World renowned Philatelist, Publisher
CLASSIFICATION: Financiers, Businessmen
SCOTT #: Antigua & Barbuda 1667

NAME: Leopold Stanislaw Kronenberg
DATES LIVED: 1812-1878
NOTED FOR: Polish-Russian Banker, Jewish &
Converted to Protestant
CLASSIFICATION: Financiers, Businessmen
SCOTT #: Poland 4036

NAME: Frank Lowy
DATES LIVED: 1930-present
NOTED FOR: Australian-Israeli Businessman
CLASSIFICATION: Financiers, Businessmen
SCOTT #: Australia 2778

BUSINESSMEN & FINANCIERS

NAME: Avram Goldfaden
DATES LIVED: 1840-1908
NOTED FOR: Businessman, 1st Yiddush Theater
CLASSIFICATION: Businessman
SCOTT #: Romania 5142A

NAME: Max Hymens
DATES LIVED: 1900-1961
NOTED FOR: French Politician & Businessman
CLASSIFICATION: Financiers, Businessmen
SCOTT #: France 2208

NAME: Sir Alfred L. Beit
DATES LIVED: 1853-1906
NOTED FOR: British Gold and Diamond Magnate
CLASSIFICATION: Businessman
SCOTT #: Rhodesia 252

BUSINESSMEN & FINANCIERS

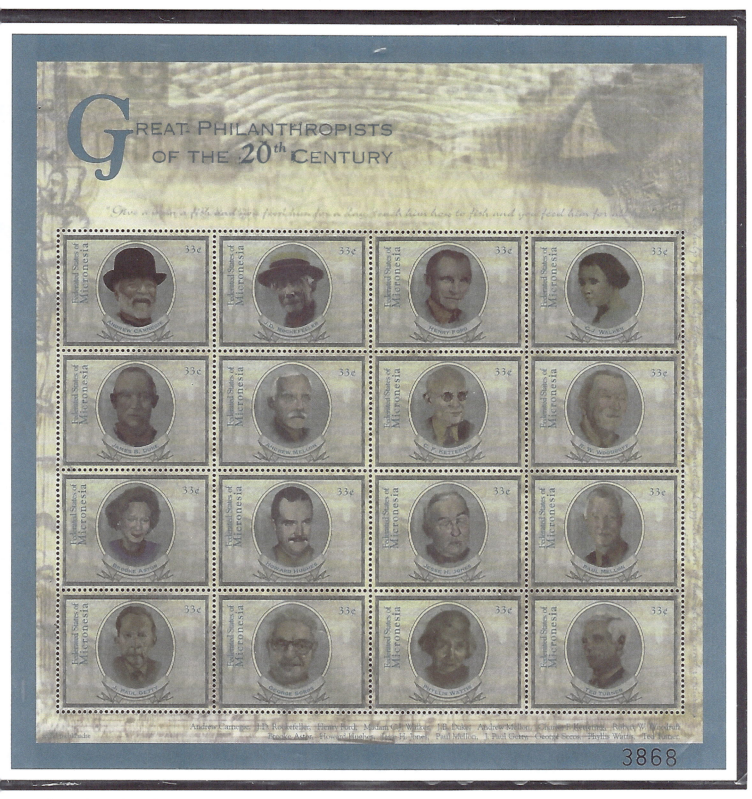

NAME: George (Gyorgy) Soros (Swartz)
DATES LIVED: 1930-present
NOTED FOR: Jewish Business Magnate, Philanthropist
CLASSIFICATION: Financiers, Businessmen
SCOTT #: Micronesia 389a-p, 389n

CHESS MASTERS

CHESS MASTERS

NAME: Antoloy Karpov
DATES LIVED: 1951-date
NOTED FOR: Chess Master
CLASSIFICATION: Chess Master
SCOTT #: Cambodia 1556

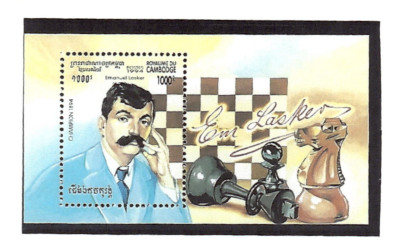

NAME: Emanuel Lasker
DATES LIVED: 1868-1941
NOTED FOR: German Chess Master
CLASSIFICATION: Chess Master
SCOTT #: Cambodia 1390 M/S

NAME: Garry Kasparov
DATES LIVED: 1963-date
NOTED FOR: Chess Master
CLASSIFICATION: Chess Master
SCOTT #: Cambodia 1557 M/S

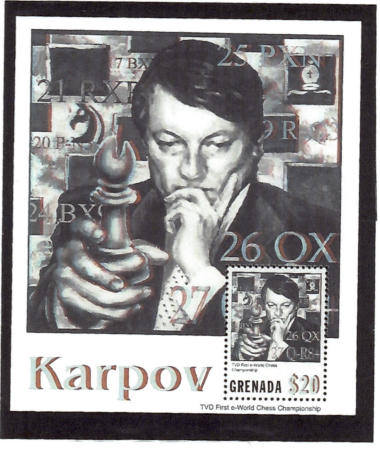

NAME: Antoloy Karpov
DATES LIVED: 1951-date
NOTED FOR: Chess Master
CLASSIFICATION: Chess Master
SCOTT #: Grenada 3385 S/S

CHESS MASTERS

NAME: Wilhelm Steinetz
DATES LIVED: 1836-1900
NOTED FOR: Austrian-American Chess Master
CLASSIFICATION: Chess Master
SCOTT #: Cambodia 1389

NAME: Wilhelm Steinitz
DATES LIVED: 1836-1900
NOTED FOR: Austrian-American Chess Master
CLASSIFICATION: Chess Master
SCOTT #: Laos 901D

NAME: Mikhail Tal
DATES LIVED: 1936-1992
NOTED FOR: Soviet-Latvia Chess Master
CLASSIFICATION: Chess Master
SCOTT #: Cambodia 1554

CHESS MASTERS

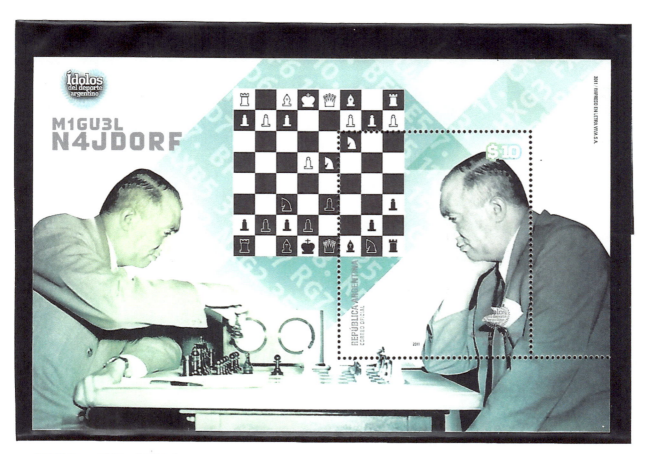

NAME: Manuel (Miguel) Najdorf
DATES LIVED: 1910-1997
NOTED FOR: born Mendel, International Chess Master
CLASSIFICATION: Chess Masters
SCOTT #: Argentina 2633

NAME: Bobby Fischer
DATES LIVED: 1943-2008
NOTED FOR: American World Chess Champion
CLASSIFICATION: Chess Masters
SCOTT #: Iceland 442

NAME: Emanuel Lasker
DATES LIVED: 1868-1941
NOTED FOR: German Chess Master, Philosopher, Mathematician
CLASSIFICATION: Chess Masters
SCOTT #: Laos 901E

COMEDIANS

COMEDIANS

NAME: Jack Benny
DATES LIVED: 1894-1974
NOTED FOR: Singer, Actor, Comedian
CLASSIFICATION: Comedian
SCOTT #: Grenada 2550

COMPOSERS, MUSICIANS

COMPOSERS & MUSICIANS

NAME: Leo Ascher
DATES LIVED: 1880-1942
NOTED FOR: Composer of Operettas
CLASSIFICATION: Composer
SCOTT #: Austria 1160

NAME: Johann Strauss
DATES LIVED: 1825-1899
NOTED FOR: Austrian Waltz Composer
CLASSIFICATION: Composer
SCOTT #: Austria 1024

NAME: Ralph Benatzky
DATES LIVED: 1884-1957
NOTED FOR: Composer of the "White Horse Inn"
CLASSIFICATION: Composer
SCOTT #: Austria 1280

NAME: Leo Fall
DATES LIVED: 1873-1925
NOTED FOR: Austrian Composer
CLASSIFICATION: Composer
SCOTT #: Austria 1021

NAME: Franz Lehar
DATES LIVED: 1870-1948
NOTED FOR: Austrian Composer of Operettas
CLASSIFICATION: Composer
SCOTT #: Austria 875

NAME: Franz Lehar
DATES LIVED: 1870-1948
NOTED FOR: Austrian Composer of Operettas
CLASSIFICATION: Composer
SCOTT #: Austria 1084

COMPOSERS & MUSICIANS

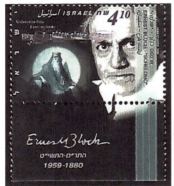

NAME: Ernest Bloch
DATES LIVED: 1880-1959
NOTED FOR: Composer
CLASSIFICATION: Composer
SCOTT #: Israel 1225

NAME: Joseph Joachim
DATES LIVED: 1831-1907
NOTED FOR: Hungarian Composer, Violinist
CLASSIFICATION: Composer
SCOTT #: Germany 9N280

NAME: Emmerich Kalman
DATES LIVED: 1882-1953
NOTED FOR: Hungarian Composer
CLASSIFICATION: Composer
SCOTT #: Austria 1226

NAME: Felix Mendelssohn
DATES LIVED: 1809-1847
NOTED FOR: Composer
CLASSIFICATION: Composer
SCOTT #: Deutch Bundenpost 4804E

NAME: Darius Milhaud
DATES LIVED: 1892-1974
NOTED FOR: Composer
CLASSIFICATION: Composer
SCOTT #: France 1975

NAME: Felix Mendelssohn
DATES LIVED: 1809-1847
NOTED FOR: Composer
CLASSIFICATION: Composer
SCOTT #: Deutchland Germany 1980

NAME: Felix Mendelsson
DATES LIVED: 1809-1847
NOTED FOR: Composer
CLASSIFICATION: Composer
SCOTT #: German Demokratic Republic 2393

NAME: Felix Mendelssohn
DATES LIVED: 1809-1847
NOTED FOR: Composer
CLASSIFICATION: Composer
SCOTT #: Monaco 2527

NAME: Felix Mendelssohn
DATES LIVED: 1809-1847
NOTED FOR: Composer
CLASSIFICATION: Composer
SCOTT #: Israel#1274

COMPOSERS & MUSICIANS

NAME: Louis Lewandowski
DATES LIVED: 1821-1894
NOTED FOR: German Composer of Synagogue
Music
CLASSIFICATION: Composer
SCOTT #: German Demokratic Republic#2845

NAME: Gustav Mahler
DATES LIVED: 1860-1911
NOTED FOR: Composer
CLASSIFICATION: Composer
SCOTT #: Austria 654

NAME: Gustav Mahler
DATES LIVED: 1860-1911
NOTED FOR: Composer
CLASSIFICATION: Composer
SCOTT #: Monaco 2571

NAME: Gustav Mahler
DATES LIVED: 1860-1911
NOTED FOR: Composer
CLASSIFICATION: Composer
SCOTT #: Czechoslavakia 3119

NAME: Gustav Mahler
DATES LIVED: 1860-1911
NOTED FOR: Composer
CLASSIFICATION: Composer
SCOTT #: Israel 1274

NAME: Gustav Mahler
DATES LIVED: 1860-1911
NOTED FOR: Composer
CLASSIFICATION: Composer
SCOTT #: Hungary 2942

NAME: Felix Mendelssohn
DATES LIVED: 1809-1847
NOTED FOR: Composer
CLASSIFICATION: Composer
SCOTT #: Bulgaria 3988c

NAME: Felix Mendelsson
DATES LIVED: 1809-1847
NOTED FOR: Composer
CLASSIFICATION: Composer
SCOTT #: German Demokratic Republic 421

COMPOSERS & MUSICIANS

NAME: Darius Milhaud
DATES LIVED: 1892-1974
NOTED FOR: Composer
CLASSIFICATION: Composer
SCOTT #: Israel 1232

NAME: Jacques Offenbach
DATES LIVED: 1819-1880
NOTED FOR: French Composer, Cellist
CLASSIFICATION: Composer
SCOTT #: Gabon C230

NAME: Ira Gershwin
DATES LIVED: 1896-1983
NOTED FOR: American Lyricist, Songwriter
CLASSIFICATION: Musician
SCOTT #: United States 3345

NAME: George Gershwin
DATES LIVED: 1898-1937
NOTED FOR: American Musician, Composer,
Pianist
CLASSIFICATION: Musician
SCOTT #: United States 3345

NAME: George Gershwin
DATES LIVED: 1898-1937
NOTED FOR: American Musician, Composer,
Pianist
CLASSIFICATION: Musician
SCOTT #: United States 1484

NAME: Porgy & Bess
DATES LIVED:
NOTED FOR: Opera By Ira & George Gershwin
CLASSIFICATION: Musician
SCOTT #: United States 2768

NAME: George Gershwin
DATES LIVED: 1898-1937
NOTED FOR: American Musician, Composer,
Pianist
CLASSIFICATION: Musician
SCOTT #: Monaco 2092

COMPOSERS & MUSICIANS

NAME: Ahad Ha'am
DATES LIVED: 1856-1927
NOTED FOR: Composer
CLASSIFICATION: Composer
SCOTT #: Israel 1290

NAME: Irving Berlin
DATES LIVED: 1888-1989
NOTED FOR: American Composer
CLASSIFICATION: Composer
SCOTT #: United States 3669

NAME: Johann Strauss
DATES LIVED: 1825-1899
NOTED FOR: Austrian Waltz Composer
CLASSIFICATION: Composer
SCOTT #: Austria 560

NAME: Richard Strauss
DATES LIVED: 1864-1949
NOTED FOR: Composer
CLASSIFICATION: Composer
SCOTT #: Austria 2507

NAME: Felix Mendelsson
DATES LIVED: 1809-1847
NOTED FOR: Composer
CLASSIFICATION: Composer
SCOTT #: German Demokratic Republic 1984 M/S

NAME: Jaques Offenbach
DATES LIVED: 1819-1880
NOTED FOR: French Composer, Cellist
CLASSIFICATION: Composer
SCOTT #: France B536

NAME: Jaques Offenbach
DATES LIVED: 1819-1880
NOTED FOR: French Composer, Cellist
CLASSIFICATION: Composer
SCOTT #: Benin 499

NAME: Jaques Offenbach
DATES LIVED: 1819-1880
NOTED FOR: French Composer, Cellist
CLASSIFICATION: Composer
SCOTT #: Benin 500

COMPOSERS & MUSICIANS

NAME: Arnold Schoenberg
DATES LIVED: 1874-1951
NOTED FOR: Composer
CLASSIFICATION: Composer
SCOTT #: Israel 1231

NAME: Artie Shaw
DATES LIVED: 1910-2004
NOTED FOR: American Jazz Composer, Band
Leader
CLASSIFICATION: Composer
SCOTT #: Dominica 1860

NAME: Johann Strauss
DATES LIVED: 1825-1899
NOTED FOR: Vienese Composer of Operas
CLASSIFICATION: Composer
SCOTT #: Austria 873

NAME: Oscar Strauss II
DATES LIVED: 1870-1954
NOTED FOR: Vienese Composer of Operas
CLASSIFICATION: Composer
SCOTT #: Austria 872

NAME: Johann Strauss II
DATES LIVED: 1825-1899
NOTED FOR: Austrian Waltz Composer
CLASSIFICATION: Composer
SCOTT #: Monaco 998

NAME: Johann Strauss
DATES LIVED: 1825-1899
NOTED FOR: Austrian Waltz Composer
CLASSIFICATION: Composer
SCOTT #: Deutchland Germany 2045

NAME: Solomon Sulzer
DATES LIVED: 1804-1890
NOTED FOR: Austrian Composer, Chazzan
CLASSIFICATION: Composer
SCOTT #: Austria 1488

NAME: Arnold Schoenberg
DATES LIVED: 1874-1951
NOTED FOR: Composer
CLASSIFICATION: Composer
SCOTT #: Austria 1001

COMPOSERS & MUSICIANS

NAME: Henry Wiensauski
DATES LIVED: 1835-1880
NOTED FOR: Polish Violinist and Composer
CLASSIFICATION: Composer
SCOTT #: Poland 795

NAME: Kurt Weill
DATES LIVED: 1900-1950
NOTED FOR: German Composer
CLASSIFICATION: Composer
SCOTT #: Grenada Grenadines 1119 S/S

NAME: Henry Wiensauski
DATES LIVED: 1835-1880
NOTED FOR: Polish Violinist and Composer
CLASSIFICATION: Composer
SCOTT #: Poland 2482

NAME: Meredith Willson
DATES LIVED: 1902-1984
NOTED FOR: American Songwriter, Playwrite,
Composer
CLASSIFICATION: Composer
SCOTT #: United States 3349

NAME: Benny Goodman
DATES LIVED: 1909-1986
NOTED FOR: Jazz & Swing Musician
CLASSIFICATION: Musician
SCOTT #: Dominica 1861

NAME: Benny Goodman
DATES LIVED: 1909-1986
NOTED FOR: Jazz & Swing Musician
CLASSIFICATION: Musician
SCOTT #: United States 3099

COMPOSERS & MUSICIANS

NAME: Harry James
DATES LIVED: 1916-1983
NOTED FOR: American Musician, Band Leader in Swing Era
CLASSIFICATION: Musician
SCOTT #: Dominica 1863

NAME: Jerome Kern
DATES LIVED: 1885-1945
NOTED FOR: Wrote Music for "Showboat"
CLASSIFICATION: Musician
SCOTT #: United States 2110

NAME: Bernard Hermann
DATES LIVED: 1911-1975
NOTED FOR: Musician
CLASSIFICATION: Musician
SCOTT #: United States 3341

NAME: Jerome Kern
DATES LIVED: 1885-1945
NOTED FOR: Musician, Writer
CLASSIFICATION: Musician
SCOTT #: United States 2767

NAME: Erich Wolfgang Korngold
DATES LIVED: 1897-1957
NOTED FOR: Musician
CLASSIFICATION: Musician
SCOTT #: United States 3344

NAME: Arturo Toscanini
DATES LIVED: 1867-1957
NOTED FOR: Italian Musician & Conductor
CLASSIFICATION: Musician
SCOTT #: Israel (2) 955

NAME: Bronislaw Haberman
DATES LIVED: 1882-1947
NOTED FOR: Czech. Musician, Violinist
CLASSIFICATION: Musician
SCOTT #: Israel 954

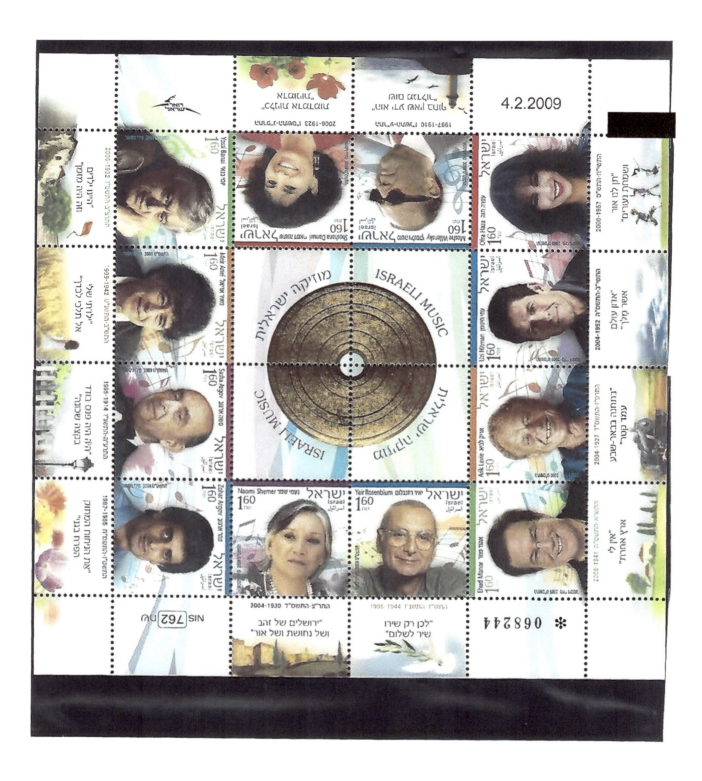

COMPOSERS & MUSICIANS

NAME: Zohar Argov
DATES LIVED: 1914-1995
NOTED FOR: Musician
CLASSIFICATION: Musician
SCOTT #: Israel 1773A

NAME: Sasha Argov
DATES LIVED: 1955-1987
NOTED FOR: Musician
CLASSIFICATION: Musician
SCOTT #: Israel 1773B

NAME: Meir Ariel
DATES LIVED: 1942-1999
NOTED FOR: Musician
CLASSIFICATION: Musician
SCOTT #: Israel 1773C

NAME: Yossi Banai
DATES LIVED: 1932-2006
NOTED FOR: Musician
CLASSIFICATION: Musician
SCOTT #: Israel 1773D

NAME: Naomi Shemer
DATES LIVED: 1930-2004
NOTED FOR: Musician
CLASSIFICATION: Musician
SCOTT #: Israel 1773E

NAME: Shoshana Damari
DATES LIVED: 1923-2006
NOTED FOR: Musician
CLASSIFICATION: Musician
SCOTT #: Israel 1773F

NAME: Yair Rosenblum
DATES LIVED: 1944-1996
NOTED FOR: Musician
CLASSIFICATION: Musician
SCOTT #: Israel 1773G

NAME: Moshe Wilensky
DATES LIVED: 1910-1997
NOTED FOR: Polish Musician, Theatre Pianist
CLASSIFICATION: Musician
SCOTT #: Israel 1773H

NAME: Ehud Manor
DATES LIVED: 1941-2005
NOTED FOR: Musician
CLASSIFICATION: Musician
SCOTT #: Israel 1773I

NAME: Arik Lavie
DATES LIVED: 1927-2004
NOTED FOR: Musician
CLASSIFICATION: Musician
SCOTT #: Israel 1773J

NAME: Uzi Hitman
DATES LIVED: 1952-2004
NOTED FOR: Musician
CLASSIFICATION: Musician
SCOTT #: Israel 1773K

NAME: Ofra Haza
DATES LIVED: 1957-2000
NOTED FOR: Musician
CLASSIFICATION: Musician
SCOTT #: Israel 1773L

COMPOSERS & MUSICIANS

NAME: Leonard Bernstein
DATES LIVED: 1918-1990
NOTED FOR: American Musician, Conductor
CLASSIFICATION: Musician
SCOTT #: Israel 1226

NAME: Leonard Bernstein
DATES LIVED: 1918-1990
NOTED FOR: American Musician, Conductor
CLASSIFICATION: Musician
SCOTT #: United States 3521

NAME: Paul Dukas
DATES LIVED: 1865-1935
NOTED FOR: French Composer
CLASSIFICATION: Musician
SCOTT #: France B389

NAME: Arthur Fielder
DATES LIVED: 1894-1979
NOTED FOR: Musician, Boston Pops
CLASSIFICATION: Musician
SCOTT #: United States 3159

NAME: Alfred Newman
DATES LIVED: 1907-1970
NOTED FOR: Musician
CLASSIFICATION: Musician
SCOTT #: United States 3343

NAME: Eugene Ormandy
DATES LIVED: 1899-1985
NOTED FOR: Hungarian Musician, Conductor
CLASSIFICATION: Musician
SCOTT #: United States 3161

NAME: Arthur Rubenstein
DATES LIVED: 1887-1982
NOTED FOR: Pianist
CLASSIFICATION: Musician
SCOTT #: Israel 935

NAME: Max Steiner
DATES LIVED: 1888-1971
NOTED FOR: Musician
CLASSIFICATION: Musician
SCOTT #: United States 3339

COMPOSERS & MUSICIANS

NAME: George Szell
DATES LIVED: 1897-1970
NOTED FOR: Hungarian-American Conductor of
Orchestra
CLASSIFICATION: Musician
SCOTT #: United States 3160

NAME: Dimitri Tiomkin
DATES LIVED: 1894-1975
NOTED FOR: Musician
CLASSIFICATION: Musician
SCOTT #: United States 3340

NAME: Arturo Toscanini
DATES LIVED: 1867-1957
NOTED FOR: Italian Musician & Conductor
CLASSIFICATION: Musician
SCOTT #: Italy 2785

NAME: Richard Tucker
DATES LIVED: 1913-1975
NOTED FOR: American Singer, Operetic
CLASSIFICATION: Musician
SCOTT #: United States 3155

NAME: Rudi Arndt
DATES LIVED: 1909-1940
NOTED FOR: Musician, Artist,
CLASSIFICATION: Musician
SCOTT #: Germany 636

NAME: Louis Gottchalk
DATES LIVED: 1829-1869
NOTED FOR: Musician, Composer, Pianist
CLASSIFICATION: Musician
SCOTT #: United States 3165

NAME: Zubin Mehta
DATES LIVED: 1936-date
NOTED FOR: India Born Musician, Conductor
CLASSIFICATION: Musician
SCOTT #: Maldive Islands 1821 M/S

COMPOSERS & MUSICIANS

NAME: Benny Goodman
DATES LIVED: 1909-1986
NOTED FOR: Jazz & Swing Musician
CLASSIFICATION: Musician
SCOTT #: St. Vincent 1144

NAME: Franz Waxman
DATES LIVED: 1906-1967
NOTED FOR: German Musician, Conductor, Film
Composer
CLASSIFICATION: Musician
SCOTT #: United States 3342

NAME: Bette Midler
DATES LIVED: 1945-date
NOTED FOR: American Singer, Actress,
Comedian
CLASSIFICATION: Musician
SCOTT #: Mali 730 M/S

NAME: E.Y. "Yipsel" Harburg
DATES LIVED: 1896-1981
NOTED FOR: Born IsidoreHochberg, Lyricist and
Songwriter
CLASSIFICATION: Composers , Musicians
SCOTT #: United States 3905

NAME: Vladimir Semyonovich Vysotsky
DATES LIVED: 1938-1980
NOTED FOR: Russian singer, songwriter, poet
CLASSIFICATION: Composers , Musicians
SCOTT #: Armenia 1056

COMPOSERS, MUSICIANS

NAME: Yehudi Menuhin
DATES LIVED: 1916-1999
NOTED FOR: American born Violinist,
Conductor, Stamp Collector
CLASSIFICATION: Composers
SCOTT #: Kyrgyzstak Sc 38, kEP M46

NAME: Robert Stolz
DATES LIVED: 1880-1980
NOTED FOR: Austrian songwriter,

Composer of operettas & film music

CLASSIFICATION: Composers
SCOTT #: San Marino 994

NAME: Annie Fischer
DATES LIVED: 1914-1995
NOTED FOR: Hungarian pianist, Composer
CLASSIFICATION: Composers
SCOTT #: Hungary 4308

COMPOSERS, MUSICIANS

NAME: Franz Lehar
DATES LIVED: 1870-1948
NOTED FOR: Austrian-Hungarian Composer,
Operettas
CLASSIFICATION: Composers , Musicians
SCOTT #: Hungary 2022

NAME: Anton G. Rubinstein
DATES LIVED: 1829-1894
NOTED FOR: Russian Pianist, Conductor, Composer
CLASSIFICATION: Composers , Musicians
SCOTT #: Russia 1745

NAME: Karl Goldmark
DATES LIVED: 1830-1915
NOTED FOR: Hungarian Composer
CLASSIFICATION: Composers , Musicians
SCOTT #: Hungary C133

CONTRIBUTORS TO WORLD CULTURE

CONTRIBUTORS TO WORLD CULTURE

NAME: Franz Kafka
DATES LIVED: 1883-1924
NOTED FOR: Writer
CLASSIFICATION: Writer
SCOTT #: Israel 1330a

NAME: George Gershwin
DATES LIVED: 1898-1937
NOTED FOR: American Musician, Composer, Pianist
CLASSIFICATION: Musician
SCOTT #: Israel 1330b

NAME: Lev Davidovich Landau
DATES LIVED: 1908-1968
NOTED FOR: Soviet Physicist
CLASSIFICATION: Scientist
SCOTT #: Israel 1330c

NAME: Albert Einstein
DATES LIVED: 1879-1955
NOTED FOR: Physicist, Mathematician
CLASSIFICATION: Scientist
SCOTT #: Israel 1330d

NAME: Leon Blum
DATES LIVED: 1872-1950
NOTED FOR: Statesman
CLASSIFICATION: Statesman
SCOTT #: Israel 1330e

NAME: Elizabeth Rachel Felix
DATES LIVED: 1821-1858
NOTED FOR: Activist
CLASSIFICATION: Human Rights
SCOTT #: Israel 1330f

CONTRIBUTORS TO WORLD CULTURE

NAME: Emile Durkheim
DATES LIVED: 1858-1917
NOTED FOR: French Socialogist
CLASSIFICATION: Socialogist
SCOTT #: Israel 1362a

NAME: Paul Ehrlich
DATES LIVED: 1854-1915
NOTED FOR: Medical Fielf of Blood Work
CLASSIFICATION: Immunologist
SCOTT #: Israel 1362b

NAME: Rosa Luxemberg
DATES LIVED: 1870-1919
NOTED FOR: Socialist Leader
CLASSIFICATION: Socialogist
SCOTT #: Israel 1362c

NAME: Norbert Wiener
DATES LIVED: 1894-1964
NOTED FOR: Mathmatic Studies
CLASSIFICATION: Mathematician
SCOTT #: Israel 1362d

NAME: Sigmund Freud
DATES LIVED: 1856-1939
NOTED FOR: Psychoanalysis Founder
CLASSIFICATION: Psychoanalist
SCOTT #: Israel 1362e

NAME: Martin Buber
DATES LIVED: 1878-1965
NOTED FOR: Philosopher
CLASSIFICATION: Philosopher
SCOTT #: Israel 1362f

CONTRIBUTORS TO WORLD CULTURE

NAME: Luis Baez di Di Torres
DATES LIVED: ?-1493
NOTED FOR: born Josef benLevi, converted to
Catholicism, Interpretor of Columbus
CLASSIFICATION: Contributors to World Culture
SCOTT #: Cuba 390

EDUCATORS, SCHOLARS

EDUCATORS & SCHOLARS

NAME: Tobias Asser
DATES LIVED: 18381913
NOTED FOR: 1911 Nobel Prize in Peace, Legal
Scholar
CLASSIFICATION: Educator, Scholar
SCOTT #: Netherlands 800

NAME: Rabbi Meir Ba'al
DATES LIVED: 139-163
NOTED FOR: Jewish Sage Scholar
CLASSIFICATION: Educator,
Scholar
SCOTT # Israel 731

NAME: Rikvah Guber
DATES LIVED: 1902-1981
NOTED FOR: Educator
CLASSIFICATION: Educator, Scholar
SCOTT #: Israel 1103

NAME: Aletta Jacobs
DATES LIVED: 1854-1929
NOTED FOR: First Woman Admitted to a University
CLASSIFICATION: Educator, Scholar
SCOTT #: Netherlands 591

NAME: Leo Rowe
DATES LIVED: 1871-1946
NOTED FOR: Doctor, Latin Educator Donor, Pan-
Amer. Dir.
CLASSIFICATION: Educator, Scholar
SCOTT #: Nicauragua C253

NAME: Jan Amos Komensky
DATES LIVED: 1592-1670
NOTED FOR: Czech Writer, Teacher, Scholar,
Educator
CLASSIFICATION: Educator, Scholar
SCOTT #: Czechoslavakia 509

NAME: Jan Amos Komensky
DATES LIVED: 1592-1670
NOTED FOR: Czech Writer, Teacher, Scholar,
Educator
CLASSIFICATION: Educator, Scholar
SCOTT #: Czechoslavakia 510

EDUCATORS & SCHOLARS

NAME: Claude Levi-Strauss
DATES LIVED: 1908-2009
NOTED FOR: French Anthropologist, Ethnologist
CLASSIFICATION: Scientists
SCOTT #: Brazil 3100

NAME: Tobias Asser
DATES LIVED: 1838-1913
NOTED FOR: Statesman & Jurist, Legal Scholar
CLASSIFICATION: Statesmen
SCOTT #: Netherlands 800

NAME: Felix Frankfurter
DATES LIVED: 1882-1965
NOTED FOR: Supreme Court Justice, Legal Scholar
CLASSIFICATION: National Government Leader
SCOTT #: United States 4422 A S/S

NAME: Louis D. Brandeis
DATES LIVED: 1856-1941
NOTED FOR: Supreme Court Justice from Prague,
Legal Scholar
CLASSIFICATION: National Government Leader
SCOTT #: United States 4422 C S/S

FILM MASTERS

FILM MASTERS

NAME: George Cukor
DATES LIVED: 1899-1983
NOTED FOR: American Film Director
CLASSIFICATION: Film Masters
SCOTT #: Hungary 3668

NAME: Gummo Marx
DATES LIVED: 1893-1977
NOTED FOR: Comedian, Actor, Movies
CLASSIFICATION: Actor
SCOTT #: Israel 1253

NAME: Harpo Marx
DATES LIVED: 1888-1964
NOTED FOR: Comedian, Actor, Movies
CLASSIFICATION: Actor
SCOTT #: Israel 1253

NAME: Danny Kaye
DATES LIVED: 1913-1987
NOTED FOR: Singer, Actor
CLASSIFICATION: Actor
SCOTT #: Israel 1253

NAME: Simone Signoret
DATES LIVED: 1921-1985
NOTED FOR: French Theatre, Movies
CLASSIFICATION: Actor
SCOTT #: Israel 1253

NAME: Chico Marx
DATES LIVED: 1887-1961
NOTED FOR: Comedian, Actor, Movies
CLASSIFICATION: Actor
SCOTT #: Israel 1253

NAME: Al Josen
DATES LIVED: 1886-1950
NOTED FOR: Singer, Theater, Movies
CLASSIFICATION: Actor
SCOTT #: Israel 1253

NAME: Peter Sellers
DATES LIVED: 1925-1980
NOTED FOR: British Theatre, Movies
CLASSIFICATION: Actor
SCOTT #: Israel 1253

FILM MASTERS

NAME: Otto Preminger
DATES LIVED: 1905-1986
NOTED FOR: Austrian-Hungarian Theatre & Film
Director
CLASSIFICATION: Film Masters
SCOTT #: Austria 2239

NAME: Fred Zinneman
DATES LIVED: 1907-1997
NOTED FOR: Austrian born Film Director,4
Academy Awards
CLASSIFICATION: Film Masters
SCOTT #: Austria 2203

NAME: Eric Pleskow
DATES LIVED: 1924-present
NOTED FOR: Film Producer, Media Executive
CLASSIFICATION: Film Masters
SCOTT #: Austria 2495

NAME: Edith Head
DATES LIVED: 1897-1981
NOTED FOR: American Famous Movie Costume
Designer, Artist
CLASSIFICATION: Film Masters
SCOTT #: United States 3772C

HOLOCAUST SURVIVORS

HOLOCAUST SURVIVORS

NAME: Simcha Holtzberg
DATES LIVED: 1924-1994
NOTED FOR: Holocaust Survivor
CLASSIFICATION: Holocaust Survivor
SCOTT #: Israel 1365

HUMAN RIGHTS ACTIVISTS

.

.

HUMAN RIGHTS ACTIVISTS

NAME: Peter Benenson
DATES LIVED: 1927-2005
NOTED FOR: English Lawyer-Founder of Human
Rights Amnesty International
CLASSIFICATION: Human Rights
SCOTT #: Denmark 790

NAME: Peter Benenson
DATES LIVED: 1927-2005
NOTED FOR: English Lawyer-Founder of Human
Rights Amnesty International
CLASSIFICATION: Human Rights
SCOTT #: Micronesia 379l

NAME: Bernath Andrei
DATES LIVED: 1908-1944
NOTED FOR: Victim of Nazi Terrorism
CLASSIFICATION: Human Rights
SCOTT #: Romania B265

NAME: Rene Cassin
DATES LIVED: 1887-1976
NOTED FOR: Nobel Prize of 1968 for Human
Rights
CLASSIFICATION: Human Rights
SCOTT #: France 2689

NAME: Jaques Bingen
DATES LIVED: 1908-1944
NOTED FOR: French Underground Resistance
CLASSIFICATION: Educator
SCOTT #: France 882

NAME: Haman Kato
DATES LIVED: 1884-1936
NOTED FOR: Hungarian Esperanto
CLASSIFICATION: Human Rights
SCOTT #: Hungary 675

HUMAN RIGHTS ACTIVISTS

NAME: Filimon Sarbu
DATES LIVED: 1916-1941
NOTED FOR: Victim of Nazi Terrorism, Anti-Faciist
CLASSIFICATION: Human Rights
SCOTT #: Romania B266

NAME: Klara Zetkin
DATES LIVED: 1857-1933
NOTED FOR: Women's Rights Activist
CLASSIFICATION: Human Rights
SCOTT #: Hungary 676

NAME: Tomas Garrigue Masaryk
DATES LIVED: 1850-1937
NOTED FOR: Lawyer, defender of Zionists and Jewish rights
CLASSIFICATION: Human Rights
SCOTT #: United States 1147

NAME: Tomas Garrigue Masaryk
DATES LIVED: 1850-1937
NOTED FOR: Lawyer, defender of Zionists and Jewish rights
CLASSIFICATION: Human Rights
SCOTT #: United States 1148

NAME: Tomas Garrigue Masaryk
DATES LIVED: 1850-1937
NOTED FOR: Lawyer, defender of Zionists and Jewish rights, 1st Pres. Of Czech.
CLASSIFICATION: National Government Leaders
SCOTT #: Czechoslovakia 247

HUMAN RIGHTS ACTIVISTS

NAME: Abbe Gregoire
DATES LIVED: 1750-1831
NOTED FOR: Established Civil Rights for Jews
in France in 1791
CLASSIFICATION: Human Rights
SCOTT #: France 2232B

INVENTORS

INVENTORS

NAME: Siegfried Samuel Marcus
DATES LIVED: 1831-1898
NOTED FOR: German Inventor - Marcus Car
CLASSIFICATION: Inventor
SCOTT #: Austria 906

NAME: L.L. Zaminhoff
DATES LIVED: 1859-1917
NOTED FOR: Polish Language Inventor of
Esperanto Language
CLASSIFICATION: Inventor
SCOTT #: Bulgaria 3231

NAME: L.L. Zamenhoff
DATES LIVED: 1859-1917
NOTED FOR: Polish Language Inventor of
Esperanto Language
CLASSIFICATION: Inventor
SCOTT #: Germany 2617 M/S

NAME: L.L. Zaminhoff
DATES LIVED: 1859-1917
NOTED FOR: Polish Language Inventor of
Esperanto Language
CLASSIFICATION: Inventor
SCOTT #: Poland 859

INVENTORS

NAME: Donat Banki
DATES LIVED: 1859-1922
NOTED FOR: Hungarian Engineer, co-invented
Carburetor
CLASSIFICATION: Inventors
SCOTT #: Hungary 4128

NAME: L.L. Zamenhoff
DATES LIVED: 1859-1917
NOTED FOR: Polish language inventor of Esperanto
Language
CLASSIFICATION: Inventors
SCOTT #: Hungary C170

NAME: Auguste Lumier
DATES LIVED: 1862-1954
NOTED FOR: Film Maker, Invented Moving Pictures
CLASSIFICATION: Inventors
SCOTT #: France 771

NAME: David (Viktor) Kaplin (Kaplan)
DATES LIVED: 1876-1934
NOTED FOR: Austria Engineer, inventor of Kaplan
turbine
CLASSIFICATION: Inventors
SCOTT #: Austria B151

NAME: Louis Lumier
DATES LIVED: 1864-1948
NOTED FOR: Film Maker, Invented Moving Pictures
CLASSIFICATION: Inventors
SCOTT #: France 771

NAME: Camilo Olivetti
DATES LIVED: 1868-1943
NOTED FOR: Inventor of the typewriter, Electrical

Engineer

CLASSIFICATION: Inventors
SCOTT #: Italy 2851 FDC

NAME: David Shwarz
DATES LIVED: 1850-1897
NOTED FOR: Inventor of 1st Aluminum

Dirigible, Croation-Hungarian

CLASSIFICATION: Inventors
SCOTT #: Cuba 3325

JNF/KKL STAMPS
JEWISH NATIONAL FUND STAMPS

JNF/KKL ISRAEL STAMPS

Chaim Weizmann - 1874-1952 , *Zionist Leader, Israeli Statesman, First President of Israel.*

1950 Yeminite End of Exile Stamp. *"Operation Magic Carpet" moved Jews living in Yemin to Israel.*

Zvi Schapira (Shapira) - 1840-1898 Russian Mathematician and Zionist. He was first to support the founding of a Jewish National Fund.

Menashe Meirovich (Meirovitch) 1860-1949, Member of "Vaad Haleumi", the Zionist National Council. A writer of many publications and books.

Theodore Herzl - 1860-1904 Commemorative stamp, Formed World Zionist Organization, Father of Modern Political Zionism.

JNF/KKL ISRAEL STAMPS

Zwi Ben Yaacov - 1922-1944

Abba Berdichev - 1924-1944

Perez Goldstein - 1923-1944

Hannah Senesh - 1921-1944

Dr. Enzo Sereni - 1905-1944

Raphael Reis - 1914-1944

Havivah Reich - 1914-1944

These soldiers were among

the "Jewish Brigade" fighting

side by side with the British

Army in World War 2. They

Parachuted into enemy territory

and lost their lives.

Israel honored them with these

stamps printed by the

Keren Kajemeth, also known as

The Jewish National Fund.

These stamps were used as

emergency stamps for the

postal service during the first

days of Israel's Independence

War, during May, 1948.

Shot during the initial break-in
Moshe Weinberg, wrestling coach
Yossef Romano, weightlifter

Shot and killed by grenade in eastern-side helicopter D-HAQO Ze'ev
Friedman, weightlifter
David Berger, weightlifter (survived grenade but died of smoke inhalation)
Yakov Springer, weightlifting judge
Eliezer Halfin, wrestler

Shot in western-side helicopter D-HAQU
Yossef Gutfreund, wrestling referee
Kehat Shorr, shooting coach
Mark Slavin, wrestler
Andre Spitzer, fencing coach
Amitzur Shapira, track coach

These stamps are a memorial issued as a dedication to the memory of the 11

Sportsmen who lost their lives at the Munich Olympics in 1972. They were issued

by the *KKL* or the *Jewish National Fund*.

JNF/KKL ISRAEL STAMPS

Chanah Senesh

This Chanah Senesh (Hannah Senesh) stamp is a contribution stamp issued in 1947 in Germany by the KKL/JNF or Jewish National Fund. It has the catalog number GE206. Hannah Szenes, anglicized as Hannah Senesh lived from 1921-1944, was a poet and a Special Operations Executive (SOE) paratrooper. She was one of 37 Jewish parachutists of Mandate Palestine, affiliated by the British Army, to rescue Hungarian Jews who were to be deported to the Auschwitz German death camp. She was arrested at the Hungarian border, imprisoned and tortured, but did not give details of her mission. She was tried and executed by a firing squad. She is regarded as a national heroine in Israel. Her poetry is recognized in Israel and has several streets named after her, as well as a kibbutz and Zionist youth movement.

JOURNALISTS

JOURNALISTS

NAME: Illes Monus
DATES LIVED: 1888-1944
NOTED FOR: Journalist- Party Leader
CLASSIFICATION: Writer
SCOTT #: Hungary B180

NAME: Agnes de Mille
DATES LIVED: 1905-1993
NOTED FOR: American Dancer & Choreographer,
Journalist
CLASSIFICATION: Journalist
SCOTT #: United States 3842

LABOR LEADERS

LABOR LEADERS

NAME: Samuel Gompers
DATES LIVED: 1850-1924
NOTED FOR: AFL-CIO Labor Union Leader
CLASSIFICATION: Labor Leader
SCOTT #: United States 988

NAME: Aharon David Gordon
DATES LIVED: 1856-1922
NOTED FOR: Laborer
CLASSIFICATION: Labor Leader
SCOTT #: Israel 1543

MAGICIANS

MAGICIANS

NAME: Harry Houdini
DATES LIVED: 1874-1926
NOTED FOR: American Magician, Illusionist
CLASSIFICATION: Magician
SCOTT #: United States 3651

NAME: David Copperfield
DATES LIVED: 1956-present
NOTED FOR: born David Seth Kotkin, Illusionist,
Magician
CLASSIFICATION: Magicians
SCOTT #: Dominica 2241

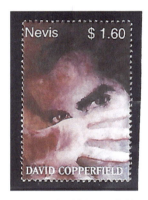

NAME: David Copperfield
DATES LIVED: 1956-present
NOTED FOR: born David Seth Kotkin, Illusionist,
Magician
CLASSIFICATION: Magicians
SCOTT #: Nevis 1229

MARTYRS

NAME: Yosef Glazman
DATES LIVED: 1908-1943
NOTED FOR: WW2 Uprissing Leader
CLASSIFICATION: Martyrs
SCOTT #: Israel (2) 841A S/S

NAME: Mordechai Anielewicz
DATES LIVED: 1919-1943
NOTED FOR: WW2 Uprissing Leader
CLASSIFICATION: Martyrs
SCOTT #: Israel 841c S/S

MARTYRS

NAME: Martyrs for Independence
DATES LIVED:
NOTED FOR: Heroes for Jewish Freedom
CLASSIFICATION: Martyrs
SCOTT #: Israel [20] 831 Sheet

NAME: Eliyahu Bet-Tzuri
DATES LIVED: 1922-1945
NOTED FOR: Martyr For Independence
CLASSIFICATION: Martyrs
SCOTT #: Israel 831A

NAME: Hannah Szenes
DATES LIVED: 1921-1944
NOTED FOR: Anti Nazi Paratropoper, Poet
CLASSIFICATION: Martyrs
SCOTT #: Israel 831B

MARTYRS

NAME: Schlomo Ben Yossi
DATES LIVED: 1913-1938
NOTED FOR: First Jew in Gallows of Palestine
CLASSIFICATION: Martyrs
SCOTT #: Israel 831C

NAME: Yoseph Lishanski
DATES LIVED: 1890-1917
NOTED FOR: Espionage Martyr
CLASSIFICATION: Martyrs
SCOTT #: Israel 831D

NAME: Naaman Belkind
DATES LIVED: 1889-1917
NOTED FOR: Martyr For Independence
CLASSIFICATION: Martyrs
SCOTT #: Israel 831E

NAME: Eliezer Kashani
DATES LIVED: 1923-1947
NOTED FOR: Martyr For Independence
CLASSIFICATION: Martyrs
SCOTT #: Israel 831F

NAME: Yechiel Dresner
DATES LIVED: 1922-1947
NOTED FOR: Martyr For Independence
CLASSIFICATION: Martyrs
SCOTT #: Israel 831G

NAME: Dov Gruner
DATES LIVED: 1912-1947
NOTED FOR: Martyr For Independence
CLASSIFICATION: Martyrs
SCOTT #: Israel 831H

NAME: Mordechai Alkachi
DATES LIVED: 1925-1947
NOTED FOR: Martyr
CLASSIFICATION: Martyrs
SCOTT #: Israel 831i

NAME: Eliahu Hakim
DATES LIVED: 1925-1945
NOTED FOR: Martyr For Independence
CLASSIFICATION: Martyrs
SCOTT #: Israel 831J

NAME: Meir Nakar
DATES LIVED: 1926-1947
NOTED FOR: Martyr For Independence
CLASSIFICATION: Martyrs
SCOTT #: Israel 831K

NAME: Avasholom Haviv
DATES LIVED: 1926-1947
NOTED FOR: Martyr For Independence
CLASSIFICATION: Martyrs
SCOTT #: Israel 831L

NAME: Yaavov Weiss
DATES LIVED: 1924-1947
NOTED FOR: Martyr For Independence
CLASSIFICATION: Martyrs
SCOTT #: Israel 831M

NAME: Meir Finestein
DATES LIVED: 1927-1947
NOTED FOR: Martyr For Independence
CLASSIFICATION: Martyrs
SCOTT #: Israel 831N

NAME: Moshe Barazani
DATES LIVED: 1921-1947
NOTED FOR: Martyr For Independence
CLASSIFICATION: Martyrs
SCOTT #: Israel 831O

NAME: Eli Cohen
DATES LIVED: 1924-1965
NOTED FOR: Martyr For Independence
CLASSIFICATION: Martyrs
SCOTT #: Israel 831P

NAME: Samuel Azaar
DATES LIVED: 1929-1955
NOTED FOR: Martyr For Independence
CLASSIFICATION: Martyrs
SCOTT #: Israel 831Q

NAME: Moshe Marzouk
DATES LIVED: 1927-1955
NOTED FOR: Martyr For Independence
CLASSIFICATION: Martyrs
SCOTT #: Israel 831R

NAME: Shalom Salih
DATES LIVED: 1934-1952
NOTED FOR: Martyr For Independence
CLASSIFICATION: Martyrs
SCOTT #: Israel 831S

NAME: Yosef Basri
DATES LIVED: 1923-1952
NOTED FOR: Martyr For Independence
CLASSIFICATION: Martyrs
SCOTT #: Israel 831T

MARTYRS

NAME: Jesus Christ
DATES LIVED: 0-32AD
NOTED FOR: Born Jewish, Savior
CLASSIFICATION: Martyrs
SCOTT #: Nicaragua 971-973

NAME: Endre Sagvari
DATES LIVED: 1913-1944
NOTED FOR: Hungarian Resistance Fighter
CLASSIFICATION: Martyrs
SCOTT #: Hungary B186

NAME: Zoltan Schonerz
DATES LIVED: 1905-1942
NOTED FOR: Engineer
CLASSIFICATION: Scientists
SCOTT #: Hungary B181

MARTYRS

These 6 stamps denote famous people who may or may not be Jewish but may have Jewish blood by their ancestry. They are noted because they believed in humanity and had strong convictions of the persecuted Jews and others who were being murdered,

These six men and one woman deserved credit to the Jewish people as "freedom fighters". They were dedicated to joining such movements as the *Social Democratic Party of Germany* (SPD) during World War 1. Other parties they were involved or associated with were the *Communist Party of Germany* (KPD), *Rote Hilfe, Rote Frontkampferbund (RFB), National Socialists, Saefkow-Jacob-Bastlein Organization, Bewegung Freis Deutshland, Kreisau , Kreisau Circle,* and the *Union of Persecutees of the Nazi Regime.* These movement groups were to fight Adolf Hitler and Nazism, and distribute flyers of opposition to them in the name of freedom. They were arrested, placed in jail, put in concentration camps, beheaded or put to death. 55 million people in Germany and Europe were wiped out and so many of them were Jews. These "Resistance fighters" put their lives on the line for community and peace, and thus, I feel they deserve credit for their good deeds, as well as many others they recruited, for their cause.

These six stamps were issued by Germany in 1964- Nazi Resistance Fighters. The Scott numbers are B112-B117.

MILITARY LEADERS

MILITARY LEADERS

NAME: Yigdal Allon
DATES LIVED: 1918-1980
NOTED FOR: Military
CLASSIFICATION: Military Leaders
SCOTT #: Israel 858

NAME: Ya'acov Dori
DATES LIVED: 1899-1973
NOTED FOR: Israeli Defense
CLASSIFICATION: Military Leaders
SCOTT #: Israel 1519

NAME: Samuel Marshall
DATES LIVED: 1900-1977
NOTED FOR: American Military Historian
CLASSIFICATION: Military Leaders
SCOTT #: Russia 5612

NAME: Joseph Trumpeldor
DATES LIVED: 1880-1920
NOTED FOR: Military Hero, Zionist
CLASSIFICATION: Military Leaders
SCOTT #: Israel 741

NAME: Joseph Trumpeldor
DATES LIVED: 1880-1920
NOTED FOR: Military Hero, Zionist
CLASSIFICATION: Military Leaders
SCOTT #: Israel 401

NAME: General Charles O. Wingate
DATES LIVED: 1903-1944
NOTED FOR: Military
CLASSIFICATION: Military Leaders
SCOTT #: Israel 881

NAME: Judas Maccabeus
DATES LIVED: 190BC-160BC
NOTED FOR: Jewish Warrior
CLASSIFICATION: Military Leaders
SCOTT #: Israel 209

NAME: Arnold Zweig
DATES LIVED: 1887-1968
NOTED FOR: German Soldier & Writer
CLASSIFICATION: Military Leaders
SCOTT #: German Demokratic Republic 2604

MILITARY LEADERS

NAME: Lev Dovatar
DATES LIVED: 1903-1941
NOTED FOR: Cossack Major General killed in WW2
CLASSIFICATION: Military Leaders
SCOTT #: Russia 862

NATIONAL GOVERNMENT LEADERS

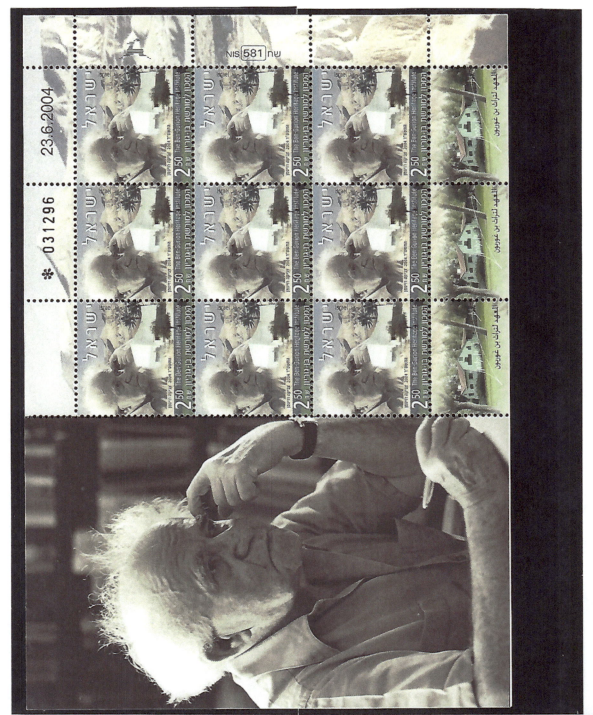

NAME: David Ben-Gurion
DATES LIVED: 1886-1973
NOTED FOR: Prime Minister of Israel
CLASSIFICATION: National Government Leader
SCOTT #: Israel (13) 1572 Sheet

NATIONAL GOVERNMENT LEADERS

NAME: Menachim Begin
DATES LIVED: 1913-1992
NOTED FOR: Prime Minister
CLASSIFICATION: National Government Leader
SCOTT #: Israel (9) 1551 SHEET

NAME: Menachim Begin
DATES LIVED: 1913-1992
NOTED FOR: Prime Minister
CLASSIFICATION: National Government Leader
SCOTT #: Israel 1551

NATIONAL GOVERNMENT LEADERS

NAME: Menachim Begin
DATES LIVED: 1913-1992
NOTED FOR: Prime Minister
CLASSIFICATION: National Government Leader
SCOTT #: Israel 1153

NAME: David Ben-Gurion
DATES LIVED: 1886-1973
NOTED FOR: Prime Minister of Israel
CLASSIFICATION: National Government Leader
SCOTT #: Israel 547

NAME: David Ben-Gurion
DATES LIVED: 1886-1973
NOTED FOR: Prime Minister of Israel
CLASSIFICATION: National Government Leader
SCOTT #: Israel 705

NAME: David Ben-Gurion
DATES LIVED: 1886-1973
NOTED FOR: Prime Minister of Israel
CLASSIFICATION: National Government Leader
SCOTT #: Israel 548

NAME: David Ben-Gurion
DATES LIVED: 1886-1973
NOTED FOR: Prime Minister of Israel
CLASSIFICATION: National Government Leader
SCOTT #: Israel 950

NAME: Moshe Dayan
DATES LIVED: 1915-1981
NOTED FOR: Minister of Defense
CLASSIFICATION: National Government Leader
SCOTT #: Israel 1000

NATIONAL GOVERNMENT LEADERS

NAME: Abba Eban
DATES LIVED: 1915-2002
NOTED FOR: Government
CLASSIFICATION: National Government Leader
SCOTT #: Israel 1652

NAME: Levi Eshkol
DATES LIVED: 1895-1969
NOTED FOR: Prime Minister of Israel
CLASSIFICATION: National Government Leader
SCOTT #: Israel 408

NAME: Benjamin Disraeli
DATES LIVED: 1804-1881
NOTED FOR: British Prime Minister
CLASSIFICATION: National Government Leader
SCOTT #: Great Britain 1190

NAME: Meir Dizengoff
DATES LIVED: 1861-1936
NOTED FOR: Mayor of Tel Aviv, Founder
CLASSIFICATION: National Government Leader
SCOTT #: Israel 919

NAME: Chaim Herzog
DATES LIVED: 1918-1997
NOTED FOR: President of Israel
CLASSIFICATION: National Government Leader
SCOTT #: Israel 1329

NAME: Bruno Kreisky
DATES LIVED: 1911-1990
NOTED FOR: Austrian Politician, Foreign Minister
CLASSIFICATION: National Government Leader
SCOTT #: Austria 1527

NATIONAL GOVERNMENT LEADERS

NAME: Yitzhak Gruenbaum
DATES LIVED: 1879-1970
NOTED FOR: Minister of Interior
CLASSIFICATION: National Government Leader
SCOTT #: Israel 754

NAME: Jacob Herzog
DATES LIVED: 1921-1972
NOTED FOR: Ambassador to Canada, Rabbi
CLASSIFICATION: National Government Leader
SCOTT #: Israel 555

NAME: Golda Meir
DATES LIVED: 1898-1978
NOTED FOR: Prime Minister of Israel
CLASSIFICATION: National Government Leader
SCOTT #: Israel 770

NAME: Louis J. Papineau
DATES LIVED: 1786-1871
NOTED FOR: Legislative member, Patriot
CLASSIFICATION: National Government Leader
SCOTT #: Canada 539

NAME: Pawel Finder
DATES LIVED: 1904-1944
NOTED FOR: Polish-Jewish Communist Leader-
1st Sec. of Polish Workers Party
CLASSIFICATION: National Government Leader
SCOTT #: Poland 2532

NAME: Yitzhak Rabin
DATES LIVED: 1922-1995
NOTED FOR: Prime Minister
CLASSIFICATION: National Government Leader
SCOTT #: Israel 1249

NATIONAL GOVERNMENT LEADERS

NAME: Yitzhak Rabin
DATES LIVED: 1922-1995
NOTED FOR: Prime Minister
CLASSIFICATION: National Government Leader
SCOTT #: Israel 1608

NAME: Pinchas Rosen
DATES LIVED: 1887-1978
NOTED FOR: Minister of Justice
CLASSIFICATION: National Government Leader
SCOTT #: Israel 974

NAME: Moshe Smoria
DATES LIVED: 1888-1961
NOTED FOR: President of Supreme Court
CLASSIFICATION: National Government Leader
SCOTT #: Israel 1023

NAME: Zalman Shazar
DATES LIVED: 1889-1974
NOTED FOR: President of Israel
CLASSIFICATION: National Government Leader
SCOTT #: Israel 571

NAME: Moshe Sharett
DATES LIVED: 1894-1965
NOTED FOR: Prime Minister of Israel
CLASSIFICATION: National Government Leader
SCOTT #: Israel 368

NAME: Walter Rathenau
DATES LIVED: 1867-1922
NOTED FOR: German-Jewish Statesman
CLASSIFICATION: National Government Leader
SCOTT #: Germany 9N86

NATIONAL GOVERNMENT LEADERS

NAME: Chaim Weizmann
DATES LIVED: 1874-1952
NOTED FOR: First President of Israel
CLASSIFICATION: National Government Leader
SCOTT #: Israel 70

NAME: Chaim Weizmam
DATES LIVED: 1874-1952
NOTED FOR: First President of Israel
CLASSIFICATION: National Government Leader
SCOTT #: Israel 71

NAME: Chaim Weizmann
DATES LIVED: 1874-1952
NOTED FOR: First President of Israel
CLASSIFICATION: National Government Leader
SCOTT #: Israel 696

NAME: Chaim Weizmann
DATES LIVED: 1874-1952
NOTED FOR: First President of Israel
CLASSIFICATION: National Government Leader
SCOTT #: Israel 353

NAME: Ezir Weizman
DATES LIVED: 1924-2005
NOTED FOR: Government
CLASSIFICATION: National Government Leader
SCOTT #: Israel 1632

NAME: Chaim Weizmann
DATES LIVED: 1874-1952
NOTED FOR: First President of Israel
CLASSIFICATION: National Government Leader
SCOTT #: Israel 354

NATIONAL GOVERNMENT LEADERS

NAME: Rachel Yanait Ben-Zvi
DATES LIVED: 1886-1979
NOTED FOR: President of Israel
CLASSIFICATION: National Government Leader
SCOTT #: Israel 1096

NAME: Yitzhak Rabin
DATES LIVED: 1922-1995
NOTED FOR: Nobel Peace Prize - 1994
CLASSIFICATION: National Government Leader
SCOTT #: St. Thomas & Prince Islands 2143 Sheet

NAME: Rechavem Ze'evy
DATES LIVED: 1926-2001
NOTED FOR: Minister of Israel
CLASSIFICATION: National Government Leader
SCOTT #: Israel 1484

NAME: Izhak Ben-Zvi
DATES LIVED: 1884-1963
NOTED FOR: President of Israel
CLASSIFICATION: National Government Leader
SCOTT #: Israel 255

NAME: Sir Julius Vogel
DATES LIVED: 1835-1899
NOTED FOR: Eighth Premier of New Zealand
CLASSIFICATION: National Government Leader
SCOTT #: New Zealand 678

NATIONAL GOVERNMENT LEADERS

NAME: Saul
DATES LIVED:
NOTED FOR: King of Israel
CLASSIFICATION: National Government Leader
SCOTT #: Israel 184

NAME: David
DATES LIVED:
NOTED FOR: King of Israel
CLASSIFICATION: National Government Leader
SCOTT #: Israel 185

NAME: Soloman
DATES LIVED:
NOTED FOR: King of Israel
CLASSIFICATION: National Government Leader
SCOTT #: Israel 186

NAME: Samson
DATES LIVED:
NOTED FOR: Last Judge of Israel
CLASSIFICATION: National Government Leader
SCOTT #: Israel 208

NAME: Bar Kokhba Simon
DATES LIVED: 132CE
NOTED FOR: Jewish Leader of Israel
CLASSIFICATION: National Government Leader
SCOTT #: Israel 210

NATIONAL GOVERNMENT LEADERS

NAME: Ion G. Duca
DATES LIVED: 1879-1933
NOTED FOR: Victim of Nazi Terrorism, Prime Minister of Romania
CLASSIFICATION: National Government Leader
SCOTT #: Romania B261

NAME: Nikolai Jorga
DATES LIVED: 1871-1940
NOTED FOR: Victim of Nazi Terrorism, Democratic Nationalist Party
CLASSIFICATION: National Government Leader
SCOTT #: Romania B263

NAME: Virgil Madgearu
DATES LIVED: 1887-1940
NOTED FOR: Victim of Nazi Terrorism, left-wing politician
CLASSIFICATION: National Government Leader
SCOTT #: Romania B262

NAME: Ilie Pintilie
DATES LIVED: 1903-1940
NOTED FOR: Victim of Nazi Terrorism, Labor Party Movement
CLASSIFICATION: National Government Leader
SCOTT #: Romania B264

NAME: Teddy Kollek
DATES LIVED: 1911-2007
NOTED FOR: Israili Politician, Jerusalem Mayor
CLASSIFICATION: National Government Leader
SCOTT #: Israel 1939

NATIONAL GOVERNMENT LEADERS

NAME: Fiorello La Guardia
DATES LIVED: 1882-1947
NOTED FOR: Mayor of New York
CLASSIFICATION: National Government Leader
SCOTT #: United States 1397

NAME: General John Monash
DATES LIVED: 1865-1931
NOTED FOR: Civil Engineer, Australian Commander
CLASSIFICATION: National Government Leader
SCOTT #: Austraila 390

NAME: Tomas Masaryk
DATES LIVED: 1850-1937
NOTED FOR: Lawyer, defender of Zionists and Jewish rights 1920-grn-blu
CLASSIFICATION: National Government Leaders
SCOTT #: Czechoslovakia 61

NAME: Raoul Wallenburg
DATES LIVED: 1912-1947
NOTED FOR: Swedish Diplomat- Saved many Jews in WW2
CLASSIFICATION: National Government Leader
SCOTT #: Hungary 4241

NAME: Gandor Fuerst
DATES LIVED: 1903-1932
NOTED FOR: Communist Party Official
CLASSIFICATION: National Government Leader
SCOTT #: Hungary B179

NAME: Kurt Eisner
DATES LIVED: 1867-1919
NOTED FOR: Politician, Bayern Prime Minister, Murdered in Munich
CLASSIFICATION: National Government Leader
SCOTT #: Bayern Sch 193

NATIONAL GOVERNMENT LEADERS

NAME: Yona Yakir
DATES LIVED: 1897-1937
NOTED FOR: General of Red Army, Victim of Stalin
CLASSIFICATION: Military
SCOTT #: Russia 3187

NAME: Franz Joseph 2nd
DATES LIVED: 1906-1989
NOTED FOR: Longest serving Prince of
Liechtenstein, marriage stamp
CLASSIFICATION: National Government Leader
SCOTT #: Liechtenstein 213

NAME: Michel Jean Pierre Debre
DATES LIVED: 1912-1996
NOTED FOR: 1st. Prime Minister of France
CLASSIFICATION: National Government Leader
SCOTT #: France 2622

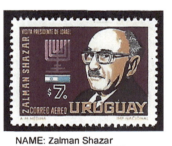

NAME: Zalman Shazar
DATES LIVED: 1889-1974
NOTED FOR: Author, Poet, President of
Israel, Politician
CLASSIFICATION: National Government Leader
SCOTT #: Uruguay C287

NAME: Jacob Sverdlov
DATES LIVED: 1885-1919
NOTED FOR: 1st. President of Russia after Revolution
CLASSIFICATION: National Government Leader
SCOTT #: Russia 5332

NAME: Franz Joseph 1st.
DATES LIVED: 1830-1916
NOTED FOR: King of Hungary,1867
CLASSIFICATION: National Government Leader
SCOTT #: Austria 150

NATIONAL GOVERNMENT LEADERS

NAME: Franz Joseph 2nd.
DATES LIVED: 1906-1989
NOTED FOR: Longest serving Prince of Lietchtenstein
CLASSIFICATION: National Government Leader
SCOTT #: Lietchtenstein 710A

NAME: Franz Joseph 2nd.
DATES LIVED: 1906-1989
NOTED FOR: Longest serving Prince of Lietchtenstein
CLASSIFICATION: National Government Leader
SCOTT #: Lietchtenstein 710B

NAME: Franz Joseph 2nd.
DATES LIVED: 1906-1989
NOTED FOR: Longest serving Prince of Lietchtenstein
CLASSIFICATION: National Government Leader
SCOTT #: Lietchtenstein 710C

NAME: Georgina von Wilczek
DATES LIVED: unknown
NOTED FOR: Wife of Franz Joseph 2nd, her great
uncle was Franz Joseph 1st.
CLASSIFICATION: National Government Leader
SCOTT #: Lietchtenstein 186

NAME: Franz Joseph 2nd.
DATES LIVED: 1906-1989
NOTED FOR: Longest serving Prince of Lietchtenstein
CLASSIFICATION: National Government Leader
SCOTT #: Lietchtenstein 185

NAME: Thomas Masaryk
DATES LIVED: 1850-1937
NOTED FOR: Lawyer, Defender of Zionists and Jewish
 Rights
CLASSIFICATION: Human Rights
SCOTT #: Czechoslovakia 91

NAME: Franz Joseph 2nd.
DATES LIVED: 1906-1989
NOTED FOR: Longest serving Prince of Lietchtenstein
CLASSIFICATION: National Government Leader
SCOTT #: Lietchtenstein 410

OTHER

OTHER

NAME: Auschwitz Berkenau
DATES LIVED:
NOTED FOR: German Concentration Camp
CLASSIFICATION: Other
SCOTT #: DDR 2294

NAME: Holocaust Memorial
DATES LIVED:
NOTED FOR:
CLASSIFICATION: Other
SCOTT #: Uruguay 1590

NAME: Flag of Israel
DATES LIVED: 1948
NOTED FOR: State of Israel Flag
CLASSIFICATION: Other
SCOTT #: Israel 15

NAME: Sverdlovsk
DATES LIVED:
NOTED FOR: City in Russia
CLASSIFICATION: Other
SCOTT #: Russia 4131

NAME: Julius Popper
DATES LIVED: 1857-1893
NOTED FOR: Romanian Engineer, Explorer
CLASSIFICATION: Other
SCOTT #: Romania 3393

NAME: Book of Genisis
DATES LIVED:
NOTED FOR: Bible
CLASSIFICATION: Other
SCOTT #: Austria 1161

OTHER

NAME: Santa Maria la Blanca Synagogue Star
of David
DATES LIVED:
NOTED FOR:
CLASSIFICATION: Other
SCOTT #: Spain (2) 2972

NAME: Maria la Blanca Synagogue Star of David
DATES LIVED:
NOTED FOR:
CLASSIFICATION: Other
SCOTT #: Spain (2) 2973

NAME: Jewish Relics
DATES LIVED: 1593
NOTED FOR: Torah Curtain Detail
CLASSIFICATION: Other
SCOTT #: Czechoslavakia 1475

NAME: Jewish Relics
DATES LIVED: 1530
NOTED FOR: Prague's Printer Emblem
CLASSIFICATION: Other
SCOTT #: Czechoslavakia 1476

NAME: Jewish Relics
DATES LIVED: 1804
NOTED FOR: Mikulev Jug
CLASSIFICATION: Other
SCOTT #: Czechoslavakia 1477

NAME: Jewish Relics
DATES LIVED: 1939-1945
NOTED FOR: Memorial for Concentration Camp
Victims
CLASSIFICATION: Other
SCOTT #: Czechoslavakia 1478

NAME: Jewish Relics
DATES LIVED:
NOTED FOR: Pincas Synagogue
CLASSIFICATION: Other
SCOTT #: Czechoslavakia 1479

NAME: Jewish Relics
DATES LIVED: 1613
NOTED FOR: Tombstone of David Gans
CLASSIFICATION: Other
SCOTT #: Czechoslavakia 1480

OTHER

NAME: Jewish Relics
DATES LIVED:
NOTED FOR: Bronze Panther Figurine
CLASSIFICATION: Other
SCOTT #: Israel 323

NAME: Jewish Relics
DATES LIVED:
NOTED FOR: Synagogue Stone Menorah
CLASSIFICATION: Other
SCOTT #: Israel 324

NAME: Jewish Relics
DATES LIVED:
NOTED FOR: Phoenician Ivory Sphinx
CLASSIFICATION: Other
SCOTT #: Israel 325

NAME: Jewish Relics
DATES LIVED:
NOTED FOR: Gold Earring
CLASSIFICATION: Other
SCOTT #: Israel 326

NAME: Jewish Relics
DATES LIVED:
NOTED FOR: Miniature Gold Capital
CLASSIFICATION: Other
SCOTT #: Israel 327

NAME: Jewish Relics
DATES LIVED:
NOTED FOR: Gold Drinking Horn
CLASSIFICATION: Other
SCOTT #: Israel 328

NAME: Israel Artifacts
DATES LIVED: 1000BC
NOTED FOR: Art Values - Jewish Relics
CLASSIFICATION: Other
SCOTT #: Israel 323-28

OTHER

NAME: Enzohayyim Sereni
DATES LIVED: 1905-1944
NOTED FOR: Executed Agent
CLASSIFICATION: Other
SCOTT #: Israel 995

NAME: Baron Maurice de Hirsch
DATES LIVED: 1831-1896
NOTED FOR: Founder of Jewish Colonization
CLASSIFICATION: Other
SCOTT #: Israel 1093

NAME: Moses Montefiore
DATES LIVED: 1784-1885
NOTED FOR: First Knighted Jew
CLASSIFICATION: Other
SCOTT #: Israel 777

NAME: Jerusalem
DATES LIVED:
NOTED FOR: Art Landscape Painting
CLASSIFICATION: Other
SCOTT #: Grenada M/S

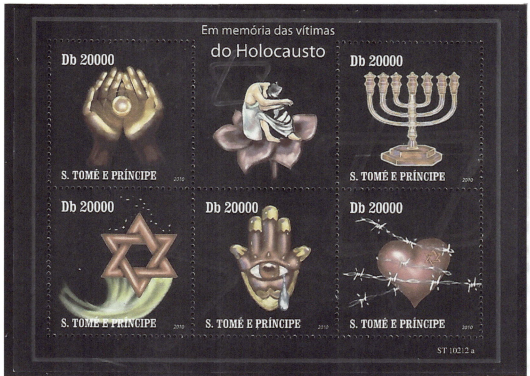

NAME: Cupped Hands
DATES LIVED: 1937-1945
NOTED FOR: Symbol
CLASSIFICATION: Other
SCOTT #: St. Thomas & Prince Islands 2245 Sheet

NAME: Star of David
DATES LIVED: 1937-1945
NOTED FOR: Symbol
CLASSIFICATION: Other
SCOTT #: St. Thomas & Prince Islands 2245 Sheet

NAME: Crying Eye
DATES LIVED: 1937-1945
NOTED FOR: Symbol
CLASSIFICATION: Other
SCOTT #: St. Thomas & Prince Islands 2245 Sheet

NAME: Menorah
DATES LIVED: 1937-1945
NOTED FOR: Symbol
CLASSIFICATION: Other
SCOTT #: St. Thomas & Prince Islands 2245 Sheet

NAME: Heart & Barbed Wire
DATES LIVED: 1937-1945
NOTED FOR: Symbol
CLASSIFICATION: Other
SCOTT #: St. Thomas & Prince Islands 2245 Sheet

NAME: Rememberance of Holocaust Victims
DATES LIVED: 1937-1945
NOTED FOR: Symbol
CLASSIFICATION: Other
SCOTT #: St. Thomas & Prince Islands 2245 Sheet

NAME: Israel-Portugal
DATES LIVED:
NOTED FOR: Joint Issue - Maritime Research with Israel
CLASSIFICATION: Other
SCOTT #: Portugal 2017 issue

NAME: Touro Synagogue
DATES LIVED: 1763-present
NOTED FOR: Oldest existing Synagogue in US, Newport, R.I.
CLASSIFICATION: Other
SCOTT #: United States 2017

NAME: Huldah
DATES LIVED:
NOTED FOR: Biblical Woman
CLASSIFICATION: Other
SCOTT #: Israel 887

NAME: Hannah
DATES LIVED:
NOTED FOR: Biblical Woman
CLASSIFICATION: Other
SCOTT #: Israel 885

NAME: Cecil Stuart Blankinship
DATES LIVED: 1904-1973
NOTED FOR: Architect, 'Habitat Stamp UN Conference'
CLASSIFICATION: Other
SCOTT #: Canada 690

NAME: Ruth
DATES LIVED:
NOTED FOR: Biblical Woman
CLASSIFICATION: Other
SCOTT #: Israel 886

Day of issue · Jour d'émission
Canada Post · Postes Canada

NAME: Canada-Israel
DATES LIVED: 2010
NOTED FOR: 60 years of Relations, 1st Day Cover
CLASSIFICATION: Other
SCOTT #: Canada 2379

Vilniaus choralinė sinagoga

NAME: Choral Synagogue
DATES LIVED:
NOTED FOR: Lithuania Synagogue in Vilnius, Still used
CLASSIFICATION: Other
SCOTT #: Lithuania New 2017 Issue

OTHER

And they shall beat their swords into plowshares, and their spears into pruning hooks. Isa. 2:4

And the work of righteousness shall be peace. Isa. 32:17

B'nai Brith salutes the Peace Corps, dedicated to peaceful relations among nations.

NAME: Peace Corps
DATES LIVED:
NOTED FOR: Special First Day Cover, Writing in

Hebrew -Shalom (Peace)

CLASSIFICATION: Other
SCOTT #: United States 1447

PHILOSOPHERS

PHILOSOPHERS

NAME: Henri Bergson
DATES LIVED: 1859-1941
NOTED FOR: French Philosopher
CLASSIFICATION: Philosopher
SCOTT #: France 934

NAME: Martin Buber
DATES LIVED: 1878-1965
NOTED FOR: Philosopher
CLASSIFICATION: Philosopher
SCOTT #: Germany 1268

NAME: Hans Kelsen
DATES LIVED: 1881-1973
NOTED FOR: Austrian Legal Philosopher,
Teacher
CLASSIFICATION: Philosopher
SCOTT #: Austria 1191

NAME: Hans Kelsen
DATES LIVED: 1881-1973
NOTED FOR: Austrian Legal Philosopher,Teacher
CLASSIFICATION: Philosopher
SCOTT #: Austria 1190

NAME: Joseph G. Klausner
DATES LIVED: 1874-1958
NOTED FOR: Historian, Philosopher
CLASSIFICATION: Philosopher
SCOTT #: Israel 804

NAME: Rabbi Moshe ben Maimon (Maimonides)
DATES LIVED: 1135-1204
NOTED FOR: Rabbi & Philosopher
CLASSIFICATION: Philosopher
SCOTT #: Israel 74

PHILOSOPHERS

NAME: Baruch Spinoza
DATES LIVED: 1632-1677
NOTED FOR: Philosopher
CLASSIFICATION: Philosopher
SCOTT #: Israel 1485

NAME: Baruch Spinoza
DATES LIVED: 1632-1677
NOTED FOR: Philosopher
CLASSIFICATION: Philosopher
SCOTT #: Netherlands 567

NAME: Rosa Luxemberg
DATES LIVED: 1871-1919
NOTED FOR: Economist, Philosopher
CLASSIFICATION: Philosopher
SCOTT #: German Demokratic Republic 419

NAME: Moses Mendelssohn
DATES LIVED: 1729-1786
NOTED FOR: Philosopher
CLASSIFICATION: Philosopher
SCOTT #: Germany 9N429

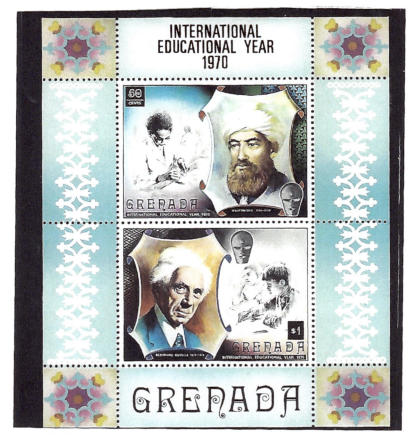

NAME: Rabbi Moshe ben Maimonadis
DATES LIVED: 1135-1204
NOTED FOR: Rabbi & Philosopher
CLASSIFICATION: Philosopher
SCOTT #: Grenada 402A S/S

PHILOSOPHERS

NAME: Moses Maimonides
DATES LIVED: 1135-1204
NOTED FOR: Philosopher, stamp is 800th Anniv. of death
CLASSIFICATION: Philosophers
SCOTT #: Grenada Grenadines 2611

NAME: Raymond Aron
DATES LIVED: 1905-1983
NOTED FOR: French Philosopher, Professor
CLASSIFICATION: Philosopher
SCOTT #: France 3837

NAME: Rosa Luxemburg
DATES LIVED: 1871-1919
NOTED FOR: Economist, Philosopher, Socialist leader
CLASSIFICATION: Philosophers
SCOTT #: Germany Ml478

NAME: Edith Stein
DATES LIVED: 1891-1942
NOTED FOR: German Philosopher, Converted to Roman Catholic
CLASSIFICATION: Philosophers
SCOTT #: Germany 1385

NAME: Ferdinand Johann Lassalle-Wolfson
DATES LIVED: 1825-1964
NOTED FOR: German-Jewish Philosopher, Socialist, Jurist, Political Activist
CLASSIFICATION: Philosophers
SCOTT #: Germany 1348

PHILOSOPHERS

NAME: Jeanne Hirsch
DATES LIVED: 1910-2000
NOTED FOR: UNESCO Director of Philosophy, Swiss
  Exec. Council Representative
CLASSIFICATION: Philosophers
SCOTT #: Switzerland 2159

NAME: Rabbi Judah Loew (Low) ben Bezael
DATES LIVED: 1526?-1609
NOTED FOR: Maharal of Prague, Talmudic Scholar,
  Philosopher
CLASSIFICATION: Philosophers
SCOTT #: Czechoslovakia 3423

POLITICIANS

POLITICIANS

NAME: Rene Blum
DATES LIVED: 1889-1967
NOTED FOR: Politician, Diplomat
CLASSIFICATION: Politician
SCOTT #: Monaco 636

NAME: Pierre Mendes France
DATES LIVED: 1907-1982
NOTED FOR: French Politician
CLASSIFICATION: Politician
SCOTT #: France 1906

NAME: Matyas Racosi
DATES LIVED: 1892-1971
NOTED FOR: Hungarian Politician
CLASSIFICATION: Politician
SCOTT #: Hungary 987

NAME: Israel Rokach
DATES LIVED: 1896-1959
NOTED FOR: Government
CLASSIFICATION: Politician
SCOTT #: Israel 1713

NAME: Matyas Racosi
DATES LIVED: 1892-1971
NOTED FOR: Hungarian Politician
CLASSIFICATION: Politician
SCOTT #: Hungary 998

NAME: Bela Kun (Kohn)
DATES LIVED: 1886-1938
NOTED FOR: Hungarian Communist
Revolutionary, Politician
CLASSIFICATION: Politician
SCOTT #: Hungary 2970

POLITICIANS

NAME: Bela Kun (Kohn)
DATES LIVED: 1886-1938
NOTED FOR: Hungarian Communist Revolutionary
Politician
CLASSIFICATION: Politician
SCOTT #: Hungary 2210

NAME: Bela Kun (Kohn)
DATES LIVED: 1886-1938
NOTED FOR: Hungarian Communist
Revolutionary, Politician
CLASSIFICATION: Politician
SCOTT #: Russia 5431

NAME: Sir Joshua Hassan
DATES LIVED: 1915-1997
NOTED FOR: Gibraltan Politician
CLASSIFICATION: Politician
SCOTT #: Gibraltar 745

NAME: Mania Shochat
DATES LIVED: 1880-1961
NOTED FOR: Russian Politician
CLASSIFICATION: Politician
SCOTT #: Israel 409

NAME: Julius Tandler
DATES LIVED: 1869-1936
NOTED FOR: Austrian Physician, Politician
CLASSIFICATION: Politician
SCOTT #: Austria 1358

POLITICIANS

NAME: Viktor Adler
DATES LIVED: 1852-1918
NOTED FOR: Austrian Politician, SDAP founder
CLASSIFICATION: Politicians
SCOTT #: Austria 1094

NAME: Cecile Brunschvicg
DATES LIVED: 1877-1946
NOTED FOR: Born CecileKahn, French Feminist
Politician
CLASSIFICATION: Politicians
SCOTT #: France 6478

NAME: Harvey Milk
DATES LIVED: 1930-1978
NOTED FOR: American Municipal Politician, openly
gay
CLASSIFICATION: Politicians
SCOTT #: United States 4906

NAME: Pierre Mendes France
DATES LIVED: 1907-1982
NOTED FOR: French Politician, Pres. Of Council of
Ministry
CLASSIFICATION: Politicians
SCOTT #: France 1906

NAME: Wilhelm Leuschner
DATES LIVED: 1890-1944
NOTED FOR: Politician- Executed in 1944
CLASSIFICATION: Politicians
SCOTT #: Germany 1606

NAME: Hans Kelson
DATES LIVED: 1881-1973
NOTED FOR: Jurist Costitution Law, Politics
CLASSIFICATION: Politicians
SCOTT #: Austria Mi1684

POLITICIANS

NAME: Monus (Brandstein) Illes
DATES LIVED: 1888-1944
NOTED FOR: Party Leader, Politician
CLASSIFICATION: Politicians
SCOTT #: Hungary 3118

NAME: Klara (Clara) Zetkin (Eisner)
DATES LIVED: 1857-1933
NOTED FOR: German Marxist Activist for Women's
Rights
CLASSIFICATION: Politicians
SCOTT #: Hungary 1307

NAME: Jacob Kaiser
DATES LIVED: 1888-1961
NOTED FOR: German Politician, Resistance Fighter
CLASSIFICATION: Politicians
SCOTT #: Germany 1545

NAME: Gyula Alpari
DATES LIVED: 1882-1944
NOTED FOR: Hungarian Communist Politician
CLASSIFICATION: Politicians
SCOTT #: Hungary 3420

NAME: Simone Annie Veil
DATES LIVED: 1927-2017
NOTED FOR: President of European Parliament,

French Lawyer
CLASSIFICATION: Politician
SCOTT #: France 1650

NAME: Gearhart Eisler
DATES LIVED: 1897-1968
NOTED FOR: German Politician
CLASSIFICATION: Politicians
SCOTT #: Germany 1854

PROHETS

PROPHETS

NAME: Jeremiah
DATES LIVED: 655 BC
NOTED FOR: Prophet & Writer
CLASSIFICATION: Prophet
SCOTT #: Vatican City 390

NAME: Ezekiel
DATES LIVED:
NOTED FOR: Prophet
CLASSIFICATION: Prophet
SCOTT #: Israel 525

NAME: Jeremiah
DATES LIVED:
NOTED FOR: Prophet
CLASSIFICATION: Prophet
SCOTT #: Israel 526

NAME: Isiah
DATES LIVED:
NOTED FOR: Prophet
CLASSIFICATION: Prophet
SCOTT #: Israel 527

PROPHETS

NAME: Joel
DATES LIVED: 1600-1100 BC
NOTED FOR: Prophet in Bible, Statue on Stamp
CLASSIFICATION: Prophet
SCOTT #: Brazil 872

PSYCHOANALISTS

PSYCHOANALISTS

NAME: Sigmund Freud
DATES LIVED: 1856-1939
NOTED FOR: Psychoanalysis Founder
CLASSIFICATION: Psychoanalist
SCOTT #: Austria 1175

NAME: Sigmund Freud
DATES LIVED: 1856-1939
NOTED FOR: Psychoanalysis Founder
CLASSIFICATION: Psychoanalist
SCOTT #: Grenada 510

NAME: Sigmund Freud
DATES LIVED: 1856-1939
NOTED FOR: Psychoanalysis Founder
CLASSIFICATION: Psychoanalist
SCOTT #: Mali 345

NAME: Sigmund Freud
DATES LIVED: 1856-1939
NOTED FOR: Psychoanalysis Founder
CLASSIFICATION: Psychoanalist
SCOTT #: Marshall Islands 627e

NAME: Sigmund Freud
DATES LIVED: 1856-1939
NOTED FOR: Psychoanalysis Founder
CLASSIFICATION: Psychoanalist
SCOTT #: Mexico 2038

RABBIS

RABBIS

NAME: Abraham Heschel
DATES LIVED: 1907-1972
NOTED FOR: American Rabbi
CLASSIFICATION: Rabbi
SCOTT #: Micronesia 370

NAME: Yehoshua ben Hananya
DATES LIVED: 1864-1945
NOTED FOR: Rabbi, Sage, Zionist
CLASSIFICATION: Rabbi
SCOTT #: Israel 730

NAME: Itzhak Kaduri
DATES LIVED: 1902-2006
NOTED FOR: Rabbi
CLASSIFICATION: Rabbi
SCOTT #: Israel 1702

NAME: Hirsch Kalischer
DATES LIVED: 1795-1874
NOTED FOR: Rabbi
CLASSIFICATION: Rabbi
SCOTT #: Israel 1743

NAME: Rabbi Isaac Kook
DATES LIVED: 1865-1935
NOTED FOR: First Chief Rabbi of Israel
CLASSIFICATION: Rabbi
SCOTT #: Israel 699

NAME: Janusz Korczak
DATES LIVED: 1879-1942
NOTED FOR: Physician, Teacher, Writer
CLASSIFICATION: Rabbi
SCOTT #: Israel 230

NAME: Rabbi Arys Levin
DATES LIVED: 1885-1969
NOTED FOR: Rabbi
CLASSIFICATION: Rabbi
SCOTT #: Israel 803

NAME: Rabbi Judah Leib Maimon
DATES LIVED: 1875-1962
NOTED FOR: Rabbi
CLASSIFICATION: Rabbi
SCOTT #: Israel 1011

NAME: Samuel Mohilewer
DATES LIVED: 1824-1898
NOTED FOR: Rabbi
CLASSIFICATION: Rabbi
SCOTT #: Israel 1742

RABBIS

NAME: Jacob Meir
DATES LIVED: 1856-1939
NOTED FOR: Rabbi
CLASSIFICATION: Rabbi
SCOTT #: Israel 1648

NAME: Chalom Messas
DATES LIVED: 1909-2003
NOTED FOR: Rabbi
CLASSIFICATION: Rabbi
SCOTT #: Israel 1695

NAME: Rabbi Ouziel
DATES LIVED: 1880-1953
NOTED FOR: Rabbi Hero
CLASSIFICATION: Rabbi
SCOTT #: Israel 700

NAME: Leo Baeck
DATES LIVED: 1873-1956
NOTED FOR: German Rabbi, Scholar, Theologian
CLASSIFICATION: Rabbi
SCOTT #: Germany 777

NAME: Rabbi Johanan
DATES LIVED: 200-279
NOTED FOR: Rabbi, Sandal Maker
CLASSIFICATION: Rabbi
SCOTT #: Israel 732

NAME: Samuel Salant
DATES LIVED: 1816-1909
NOTED FOR: Rabbi
CLASSIFICATION: Rabbi
SCOTT #: Israel 1647

NAME: Chatam Sofer
DATES LIVED: 1762-1839
NOTED FOR: Rabbi, Teacher
CLASSIFICATION: Rabbi
SCOTT #: Slovakia 196

NAME: Rabbi Solomon Elijah ben Zalman
DATES LIVED: 1720-1797
NOTED FOR: Rabbi
CLASSIFICATION: Rabbi
SCOTT #: Israel 1304

RABBIS

NAME: Moshe Avigdor Amiel
DATES LIVED: 1883-1945
NOTED FOR: Rabbi
CLASSIFICATION: Rabbi
SCOTT #: Israel 969

NAME: Rabbi Hayyim Joseph ben Azulai
DATES LIVED: 1724-1806
NOTED FOR: Rabbi
CLASSIFICATION: Rabbi
SCOTT #: Israel 1110

NAME: Rabbi Meir Bar-Ilan
DATES LIVED: 1880-1949
NOTED FOR: Rabbi, Founder of Movement
CLASSIFICATION: Rabbi
SCOTT #: Israel 855

NAME: Rabbi Hayyim Joseph ben Elijah
DATES LIVED: 1834-1909
NOTED FOR: Rabbi
CLASSIFICATION: Rabbi
SCOTT #: Israel 1111

NAME: Rabbi Shimon Hakham
DATES LIVED: 1843-1910
NOTED FOR: Rabbi who Promoted Literacy
CLASSIFICATION: Rabbi
SCOTT #: Israel 1087

NAME: Jacob Saul Eliachar
DATES LIVED: 1817-1906
NOTED FOR: Rabbi
CLASSIFICATION: Rabbi
SCOTT #: Israel 1646

NAME: Abraham Zacuto
DATES LIVED: 1452-1515
NOTED FOR: Rabbi
CLASSIFICATION: Rabbi
SCOTT #: Sierre Leone 91
0

RABBIS

NAME: Albert Guigui
DATES LIVED: 1944-present
NOTED FOR: Chief Rabbi of Brussels, 1st Rabbi on
Belgian stamp
CLASSIFICATION: Rabbis
SCOTT #: Belgium 2802

NAME: Louis Schwimmer
DATES LIVED: 1900-1975
NOTED FOR: Designed the 4 Chaplains US Stamp,
1st. US stamp with Jewish Person
CLASSIFICATION: Artists, Painters
SCOTT #: United States 956

SCIENTISTS

.

SCIENTISTS

NAME: Aaron Aaronsohn
DATES LIVED: 1876-1919
NOTED FOR: Botonist, Agronomist
CLASSIFICATION: Scientist
SCOTT #: Israel 742

NAME: Saul Adler
DATES LIVED: 1895-1966
NOTED FOR: Scientist
CLASSIFICATION: Scientist
SCOTT #: Israel 1202

NAME: Robert Barany
DATES LIVED: 1876-1936
NOTED FOR: Austrian-Hungarian Otologist,
Nobel in Philosophy, Medicine
CLASSIFICATION: Scientist
SCOTT #: Austria 1031

NAME: Robert Barany
DATES LIVED: 1876-1936
NOTED FOR: Austrian-Hungarian Otologist,
Nobel in Philosophy, Medicine
CLASSIFICATION: Scientist
SCOTT #: Sweden 1105

NAME: Adolph Von Bayer
DATES LIVED: 1835-
NOTED FOR: German Chemist-Nobel Prize in 1905
CLASSIFICATION: Scientist
SCOTT #: Sweden 689

NAME: Neils Bohr
DATES LIVED: 1885-1962
NOTED FOR: Danish Physicist- Nobel Prize in
1922
CLASSIFICATION: Scientist
SCOTT #: Denmark 409 & 410

NAME: Neils Bohr
DATES LIVED: 1885-1962
NOTED FOR: Danish Physicist- Nobel Prize in 1922
CLASSIFICATION: Scientist
SCOTT #: Denmark 409 A & 410 A Phosphorus

SCIENTISTS

NAME: Paul Ehrlich
DATES LIVED: 1854-1932
NOTED FOR: American Biologist & Educator
CLASSIFICATION: Scientist
SCOTT #: Germany 722

NAME: Paul Ehrlich
DATES LIVED: 1854-1932
NOTED FOR: American Biologist & Educator
CLASSIFICATION: Scientist
SCOTT #: Gambia 909

NAME: Paul Ehrlich
DATES LIVED: 1854-1932
NOTED FOR: American Biologist & Educator
CLASSIFICATION: Scientist
SCOTT #: Sweden 805 Hor. Coil

NAME: Paul Ehrlich
DATES LIVED: 1854-1932 -
NOTED FOR: American Biologist & Educator
CLASSIFICATION: Scientist
SCOTT #: Sweden 805 Vert. Coil

NAME: Paul Ehrlich
DATES LIVED: 1854-1932
NOTED FOR: American Biologist & Educator
CLASSIFICATION: Scientist
SCOTT #: Sweden (2) 805 Booklet

NAME: Mordechai Haffkine
DATES LIVED: 1860-1930
NOTED FOR: Developed Cholera Vaccine
CLASSIFICATION: Scientist
SCOTT #: Israel 1196

NAME: Leo Fizikus (Szilard)
DATES LIVED: 1898-1964
NOTED FOR: Physicist, Atomic Reactors
CLASSIFICATION: Scientist
SCOTT #: Hungary 3592

SCIENTISTS

NAME: Fritz Haber
DATES LIVED: 1868-1934
NOTED FOR: German Chemist, Nobel Recipient 1918
CLASSIFICATION: Scientist
SCOTT #: Sweden 1271

NAME: Abraham Joffe
DATES LIVED: 1880-1960
NOTED FOR: Russian Scientist, Chemist
CLASSIFICATION: Scientist
SCOTT #: Russia 4870

NAME: Aharon Katchalsky-Katzir
DATES LIVED: 1913-1972
NOTED FOR: Chemist
CLASSIFICATION: Scientist
SCOTT #: Israel 1166

NAME: Gabriel Lippman
DATES LIVED: 1845-1921
NOTED FOR: French Physicist & Inventor, Nobel in Physics
CLASSIFICATION: Scientist
SCOTT #: Sweden 804

NAME: Gabriel Lippman
DATES LIVED: 1845-1921
NOTED FOR: French Physicist & Inventor, Nobel in Physics
CLASSIFICATION: Scientist
SCOTT #: Sweden 804A

NAME: Otto Loewi
DATES LIVED: 1873-1961
NOTED FOR: German Pharmacologist
CLASSIFICATION: Scientist
SCOTT #: Austria 942

NAME: Gabriel Lippman
DATES LIVED: 1845-1921
NOTED FOR: French Physicist & Inventor, Nobel in Physics
CLASSIFICATION: Scientist
SCOTT #: Sweden 806

NAME: Gabriel Lippman
DATES LIVED: 1845-1921
NOTED FOR: French Physicist & Inventor, Nobel in Physics
CLASSIFICATION: Scientist
SCOTT #: Sweden 806A

SCIENTISTS

NAME: Lise Meitner
DATES LIVED: 1878-1968
NOTED FOR: Austrian Physicist -Radioactive Physics
CLASSIFICATION: Scientist
SCOTT #: Austria 1093

NAME: Elle Metchenikof
DATES LIVED: 1845-1916
NOTED FOR: Russian Scientist, Biologist
CLASSIFICATION: Scientist
SCOTT #: Russia 6000

NAME: Albert Micheson
DATES LIVED: 1852-1931
NOTED FOR: American Physicist, Studied Speed o
Light
CLASSIFICATION: Scientist
SCOTT #: Sweden 769

NAME: Elle Metchenikof
DATES LIVED: 1845-1916
NOTED FOR: Russian Scientist, Biologist
CLASSIFICATION: Scientist
SCOTT #: France B398

NAME: Adam Politzer
DATES LIVED: 1835-1920
NOTED FOR: 20th Century Otology Studies
CLASSIFICATION: Scientist
SCOTT #: Austria 1326

NAME: Giulio Racah
DATES LIVED: 1909-1965
NOTED FOR: Physicist
CLASSIFICATION: Scientist
SCOTT #: Israel 1165

SCIENTISTS

NAME: Albert Sabin
DATES LIVED: 1906-1933
NOTED FOR: American Medical Researcher,
Polio Vaccine
CLASSIFICATION: Scientist
SCOTT #: Brazil 2467

NAME: Jonus Salk
DATES LIVED: 1914-1995
NOTED FOR: American Medical Researcher, Polio
Vaccine
CLASSIFICATION: Scientist
SCOTT #: Tanzania 1479

NAME: Otto Warburg
DATES LIVED: 1883-1970
NOTED FOR: German Physiologist, Botanist
CLASSIFICATION: Scientist
SCOTT #: Germany 1400

NAME: Jonus Salk
DATES LIVED: 1914-1995
NOTED FOR: American Medical Researcher,
Polio Vaccine
CLASSIFICATION: Scientist
SCOTT #: Transkei 261

NAME: Richard Willstatter
DATES LIVED: 1872-1942
NOTED FOR: German Organic Chemist
CLASSIFICATION: Scientist
SCOTT #: Sweden 1150

NAME: Alfred Freid
DATES LIVED: 1864-1921
NOTED FOR: Austrian Publicist, Nobel Prize,
Psychoanalsis Founders
CLASSIFICATION: Scientist
SCOTT #: Austria 1484

SCIENTISTS

NAME: Georg Brandes
DATES LIVED: 1842-1927
NOTED FOR: Danish Physicist- Nobel Prize in 1922
CLASSIFICATION: Scientist
SCOTT #: Denmark 486

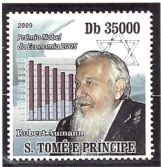

NAME: Robert Aumann
DATES LIVED: 1930-date
NOTED FOR: Economics Nobel Prize - 2005
CLASSIFICATION: Scientist, Mathematician
SCOTT #: St. Thomas & Prince Islands 2143 Sheet

NAME: Martin Chalfie
DATES LIVED: 1947-date
NOTED FOR: Chemistry Nobel Prize - 2008
CLASSIFICATION: Scientist, Chemist
SCOTT #: St. Thomas & Prince Islands 2143 Sheet

NAME: Andrew Fire
DATES LIVED: 1959-date
NOTED FOR: Physiology Nobel Prize - 2006
CLASSIFICATION: Scientist, Biologist
SCOTT #: St. Thomas & Prince Islands 2143 Sheet

NAME: Sander Koranyi
DATES LIVED: 1866-1944
NOTED FOR: Hungarian Doctor
CLASSIFICATION: Scientist
SCOTT #: Hungary 2276

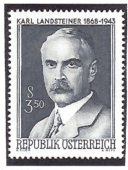

NAME: Karl Landsteiner
DATES LIVED: 1868-1943
NOTED FOR: Medicine, Virology, Born Jewish
CLASSIFICATION: Scientist
SCOTT #: Austria 813

SCIENTISTS

NAME: Albert Einstein
DATES LIVED: 1879-1955
NOTED FOR: Physicist, Mathematician
CLASSIFICATION: Scientist
SCOTT #: Mongolia (9) 2451-59 S/S

NAME: Albert Einstein
DATES LIVED: 1879-1955
NOTED FOR: Physicist, Mathematician
CLASSIFICATION: Scientist
SCOTT #: San Marino 947

SCIENTISTS

NAME: Albert Einstein
DATES LIVED: 1879-1955
NOTED FOR: Physicist, Mathematician
CLASSIFICATION: Scientist
SCOTT #: United States 1285

NAME: Albert Einstein
DATES LIVED: 1879-1955
NOTED FOR: Physicist, Mathematician
CLASSIFICATION: Scientist
SCOTT #: Israel 1609

NAME: Albert Einstein
DATES LIVED: 1879-1955
NOTED FOR: Physicist, Mathematician
CLASSIFICATION: Scientist
SCOTT #: United States 1774

NAME: Albert Einstein
DATES LIVED: 1879-1955
NOTED FOR: Physicist, Mathematician
CLASSIFICATION: Scientist
SCOTT #: Germany 1299

NAME: Albert Einstein
DATES LIVED: 1879-1955
NOTED FOR: Physicist, Mathematician
CLASSIFICATION: Scientist
SCOTT #: Marshall Islands 627i

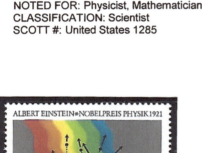

NAME: Albert Einstein
DATES LIVED: 1879-1955
NOTED FOR: Physicist, Mathematician
CLASSIFICATION: Scientist
SCOTT #: France 3112

NAME: Albert Einstein
DATES LIVED: 1879-1955
NOTED FOR: Physicist, Mathematician
CLASSIFICATION: Scientist
SCOTT #: Togo C381

SCIENTISTS

NAME: Albert Einstein
DATES LIVED: 1879-1955
NOTED FOR: Physicist, Mathematician
CLASSIFICATION: Scientist
SCOTT #: Togo C384

NAME: Albert Einstein
DATES LIVED: 1879-1955
NOTED FOR: Physicist, Mathematician
CLASSIFICATION: Scientist
SCOTT #: Togo 1021

NAME: Albert Einstein
DATES LIVED: 1879-1955
NOTED FOR: Physicist, Mathematician
CLASSIFICATION: Scientist
SCOTT #: Togo 1022

NAME: Albert Einstein
DATES LIVED: 1879-1955
NOTED FOR: Physicist, Mathematician
CLASSIFICATION: Scientist
SCOTT #: Israel 117

NAME: Albert Einstein
DATES LIVED: 1879-1955
NOTED FOR: Physicist, Mathematician
CLASSIFICATION: Scientist
SCOTT #: Sierre Leone 1847 S/S

SCIENTISTS

NAME: Albert Einstein
DATES LIVED: 1879-1955
NOTED FOR: Physicist, Mathematician
CLASSIFICATION: Scientist
SCOTT #: Russia 4741

NAME: Albert Einstein
DATES LIVED: 1879-1955
NOTED FOR: Physicist, Mathematician
CLASSIFICATION: Scientist
SCOTT #: Italy 2048

NAME: Albert Einstein
DATES LIVED: 1879-1955
NOTED FOR: Physicist, Mathematician
CLASSIFICATION: Scientist
SCOTT #: Mexico C592

NAME: Albert Einstein
DATES LIVED: 1879-1955
NOTED FOR: Physicist, Mathematician
CLASSIFICATION: Scientist
SCOTT #: Sweden 1387

NAME: Albert Einstein
DATES LIVED: 1879-1955
NOTED FOR: Physicist, Mathematician
CLASSIFICATION: Scientist
SCOTT #: Paraguay 875

NAME: Albert Einstein
DATES LIVED: 1879-1955
NOTED FOR: Physicist, Mathematician
CLASSIFICATION: Scientist
SCOTT #: Paraguay 877

SCIENTISTS

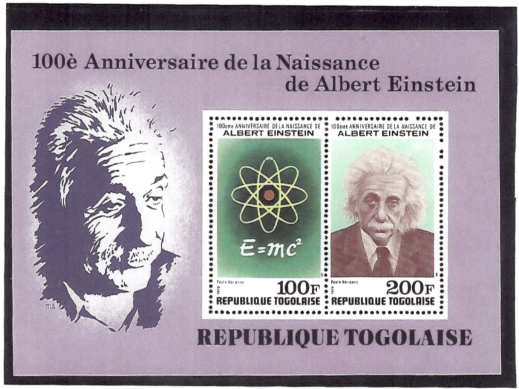

NAME: Albert Einstein
DATES LIVED: 1879-1955
NOTED FOR: Physicist, Mathematician
CLASSIFICATION: Scientist
SCOTT #: Togo 382-3 S/S

NAME: Albert Einstein
DATES LIVED: 1879-1955
NOTED FOR: Physicist, Mathematician
CLASSIFICATION: Scientist
SCOTT #: Togo (2) C380 S/S

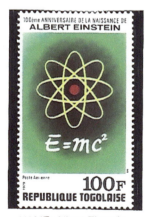

NAME: Albert Einstein
DATES LIVED: 1879-1955
NOTED FOR: Physicist, Mathematician
CLASSIFICATION: Scientist
SCOTT #: Togo C382

NAME: Albert Einstein
DATES LIVED: 1879-1955
NOTED FOR: Physicist, Mathematician
CLASSIFICATION: Scientist
SCOTT #: Togo C383

171

SCIENTISTS

NAME: Albert Einstein
DATES LIVED: 1879-1955
NOTED FOR: Physicist, Mathematician
CLASSIFICATION: Scientist
SCOTT #: Monaco 2371

NAME: Albert Einstein
DATES LIVED: 1879-1955
NOTED FOR: Physicist, Mathematician
CLASSIFICATION: Scientist
SCOTT #: Swaziland 438

NAME: Selman Waksman
DATES LIVED: 1888-1973
NOTED FOR: Ukranian - American Inventor
CLASSIFICATION: Scientists
SCOTT #: Gambia 910

NAME: Lise Meitner
DATES LIVED: 1878-1968
NOTED FOR: Austrian Physicist -Radioactive Physics
CLASSIFICATION: Scientist
SCOTT #: Austria 1093

NAME: Robert Barany
DATES LIVED: 1876-1936
NOTED FOR: Austrian-Hungarian Otologist, Nobel
in Philosophy, Medicine
CLASSIFICATION: Scientists
SCOTT #: Hungary 3155

NAME: Heinrich Hertz
DATES LIVED: 1857-1894
NOTED FOR: Grandfather Jewish, Physicist
CLASSIFICATION: Scientists
SCOTT #: Germany 354

SCIENTISTS

NAME: Dr. Jonas Salk
DATES LIVED: 1914-1995
NOTED FOR: Co-Inventor of Polio Vaccine, researcher
CLASSIFICATION: Scientists
SCOTT #: Dominica 2004

NAME: Mileva Maric
DATES LIVED: 1875-1948
NOTED FOR: married Einstein, Serbian Physicist, Never Converted
CLASSIFICATION: Scientists
SCOTT #: Serbia 660

NAME: Dr. Christian Barnard
DATES LIVED: 1922-2001
NOTED FOR: So. African 1st. Heart Transplant, Physician
CLASSIFICATION: Scientists
SCOTT #: Dominica 2001

NAME: Ida Holz Bard
DATES LIVED: 1935-present
NOTED FOR: Engineering and Computer Science Professor
CLASSIFICATION: Scientists
SCOTT #: Uruguay 2529

NAME: Richard Feynman
DATES LIVED: 1918-1988
NOTED FOR: Theoretical Physicist - Quantum Mechanics
CLASSIFICATION: Scientists
SCOTT #: United States 3909

NAME: Dr. Adam Politzer
DATES LIVED: 1835-1920
NOTED FOR: Hungarian-Austrian Physician
CLASSIFICATION: Scientists
SCOTT #: Austria 1326

NAME: Sidney Altman
DATES LIVED: 1939-present
NOTED FOR: Canadian-American molecular biologist
CLASSIFICATION: Scientists
SCOTT #: Antigua & Barbuda 2518D

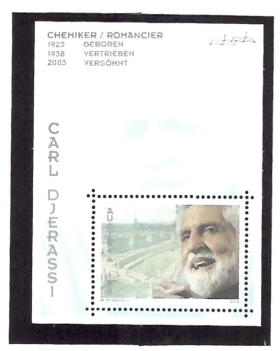

NAME: Carl Djerassi
DATES LIVED: 1923-2015
NOTED FOR: Bulgarian World Reknowned Chemist,
Oral Contraceptive
CLASSIFICATION: Scientists
SCOTT #: Austria 1990

NAME: Frigyes Koranyi
DATES LIVED: 1828-1913
NOTED FOR: Hungarian Physician, family name
Kornfeldt
CLASSIFICATION: Scientists
SCOTT #: Hungary 1498

NAME: James Franck
DATES LIVED: 1882-1964
NOTED FOR: mother Jewish, Physicist, Nobel
winner
CLASSIFICATION: Scientists
SCOTT #: Germany 1381

NAME: Frigyes Koranyi
DATES LIVED: 1828-1913
NOTED FOR: Hungarian Physician, family name
Kornfeldt
CLASSIFICATION: Scientists
SCOTT #: Hungary 1103

NAME: Lise Meitner
DATES LIVED: 1878-1968
NOTED FOR: Austrian Swedish Physicist
CLASSIFICATION: Scientists
SCOTT #: Germany 9N524

NAME: Paul C. Polanyi
DATES LIVED: 1929-present
NOTED FOR: Chemist, Nobel Prize Winner
CLASSIFICATION: Scientists
SCOTT #: Canada 489 FDC

SCIENTISTS

NAME: John Von Neuman
DATES LIVED: 1903-1957
NOTED FOR: Hungarian-American Mathematician, Physicist, Inventor
CLASSIFICATION: Scientists
SCOTT #: United States 3908

NAME: Antoine Portal
DATES LIVED: 1742-1832
NOTED FOR: French Doctor,Historian, Anotomist, Founded Royal Academy-Medicine
CLASSIFICATION: Scientist
SCOTT #: France 1699

NAME: Paul C. Polanyi
DATES LIVED: 1929-present
NOTED FOR: Chemist, Nobel Prize Winner
CLASSIFICATION: Scientists
SCOTT #: Canada 468 Bklt.

SCIENTISTS

Dr. A. S. Wiener, as co-discoverer of the Rh factor, opened a new chapter in the history of blood grouping and transfusion. In the elaboration of the significance of Rh factor in causing erythroblastosis, he not only laid the basis for the cure of this disease but opened a new era in thinking about blood disease.

NAME: Alexander S. Wiener
DATES LIVED: 1907-1976
NOTED FOR: New York leader in forensic medicine,

discovered Rh blood factor

CLASSIFICATION: Scientists
SCOTT #: United States 1425

NAME: Paul Samuelson
DATES LIVED: 1915-2009
NOTED FOR: Economics Nobel Prize Winner
CLASSIFICATION: Scientists
SCOTT #: Guine-Bissau 2837 M/S

NAME: Ernst Mahr
DATES LIVED: 1887-1930
NOTED FOR: Leading Biologist, Taxonomist, Historian
CLASSIFICATION: Scientists
SCOTT #: East Germany 1852 FDC

SOCIALISTS

SOCIALISTS

NAME: Victor Adler
DATES LIVED: 1852-1918
NOTED FOR: Socialist, Politician
CLASSIFICATION: Socialist
SCOTT #: Austria #1094

NAME: Otto Bauer
DATES LIVED: 1881-1938
NOTED FOR: Austrian Social Democrat
CLASSIFICATION: Socialist
SCOTT #: Austria #1186

SOCIOLOGISTS

SOCIOLOGISTS

NAME: Raymond Aron
DATES LIVED: 1905-1983
NOTED FOR: French Philosopher,Sociologist,
Journalist
CLASSIFICATION: Philosophers
SCOTT #: France 3152

NAME: Franz Oppenheimer
DATES LIVED: 1864-1943
NOTED FOR: German Sociologist, Political
Economist, Writer of the States
CLASSIFICATION: Sociologists
SCOTT #: Germany 837

NAME: Karl H. Marx
DATES LIVED: 1818-1883
NOTED FOR: Inventor of Marxism, Philosopher,
Sociologist, 60kon
CLASSIFICATION: Sociologists
SCOTT #: Russia 2057

NAME: Karl H. Marx
DATES LIVED: 1818-1883
NOTED FOR: Inventor of Marxism, Philosopher,
Sociologist- 1pye
CLASSIFICATION: Sociologists
SCOTT #: Russia 2058

SOCIOLOGISTS

NAME: Leo Frankel
DATES LIVED: 1844-1896
NOTED FOR: Hungarian Sociologist
CLASSIFICATION: Sociologists
SCOTT #: Hungary 938

NAME: Karl H. Marx
DATES LIVED: 1818-1883
NOTED FOR: Inventor of Marxism, Philosopher,
Sociologist
CLASSIFICATION: Sociologists
SCOTT #: Cuba 2564

SPECIAL ISSUES

NAME: Daniel & The Lion
DATES LIVED:
NOTED FOR: Bible Story on Stamps - 25 Stamps
CLASSIFICATION: Special Issues
SCOTT #: Guyana (25) 2836

Now the Lord had prepared a great fish to swallow up Jonah.

Jonah 1:17

Jonah and the Whale

NAME: Jonah & Whale
DATES LIVED:
NOTED FOR: Jonah & The Whale Story with
Stamps - 25 Stamps
CLASSIFICATION: Special Issues
SCOTT #: Palau (25) 321 S/S

THE STORY OF JOSEPH

Joseph is sold to the Ishmaelites.

Joseph is reunited with his brothers.

Joseph's brothers take his coat and cast him into a pit.

Joseph interprets Pharoah's dreams.

Jacob made Joseph a coat of many colors.

Joseph is accused by Potiphar's wife and thrown into prison.

"Joseph said unto his brethren, Come near to me...I am Joseph your brother, whom you sold unto Egypt. Now, therefore, be not grieved ...for God did send me before you to preserve life." Genesis 45

Bryna Waldman

NAME: Story of Joseph
DATES LIVED: 1100BC
NOTED FOR: Coat of many colors
CLASSIFICATION: Special Issues
SCOTT #: Guyana (24) 2834 Sheet

NAME: Noah's Ark
DATES LIVED: 2900BC
NOTED FOR: Noah's Ark
CLASSIFICATION: Special Issues
SCOTT #: St. Vincent (25) 1152a-y

NAME: Red Sea Parting
DATES LIVED:
NOTED FOR: Parting off ther Red Sea Story on Stamps - 24
CLASSIFICATION: Special Issues
SCOTT #: Guyana (24) 1994 Sheet

DAVID AND GOLIATH

*And all this assembly shall know that
the Lord saveth not the sword and spear:
for the battle is the Lord's, and he
will give you into our hands.*

Samuel chapter 17 verse 47

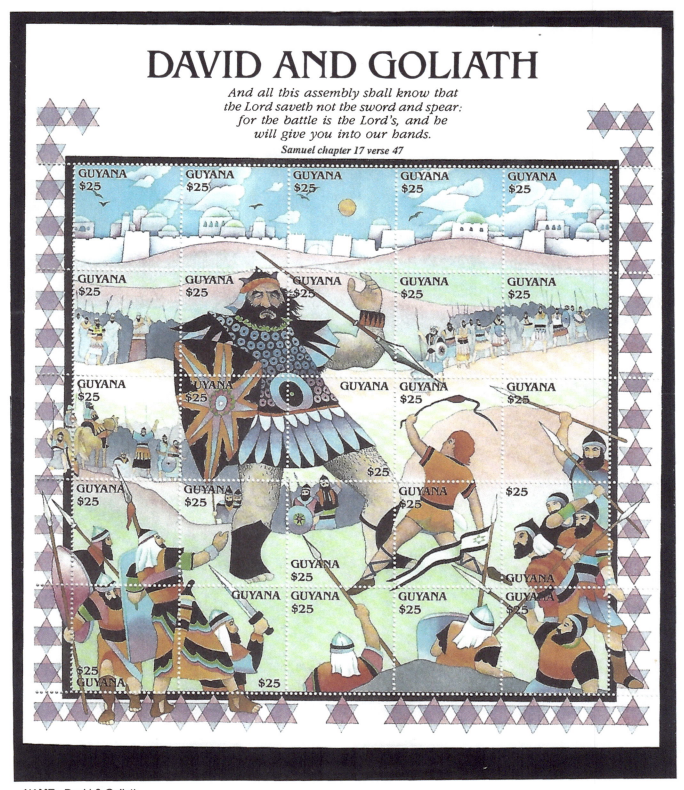

NAME: David & Goliath
DATES LIVED: 1010Bc
NOTED FOR: Bible Story David Slays
Goliath
CLASSIFICATION: Special Issues
SCOTT #: Guyana (25) 2651 Sheet

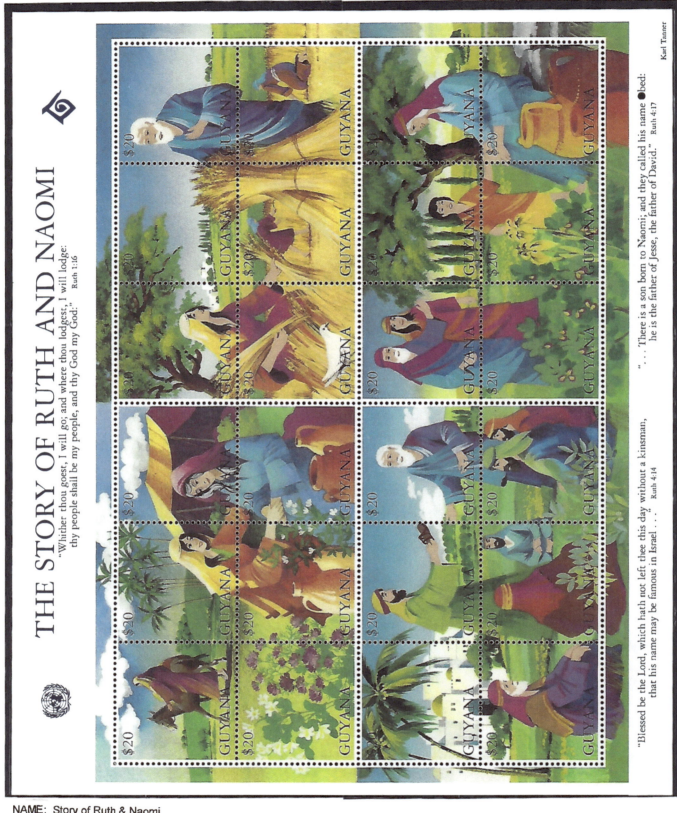

THE STORY OF RUTH AND NAOMI

"Whither thou goest, I will go; and where thou lodgest, I will lodge: thy people shall be my people, and thy God my God." Ruth 1:16

". . . 'There is a son born to Naomi; and they called his name Obed: he is the father of Jesse, the father of David." Ruth 4:17

"Blessed be the Lord, which hath not left thee this day without a kinsman, that his name may be famous in Israel . . ." Ruth 4:14

Karl Tanner

NAME: Story of Ruth & Naomi
DATES LIVED: 1100BC
NOTED FOR: Biblical Story With Stamps - 24 stamps
CLASSIFICATION: Special Issues
SCOTT #: Guyana (24) 1994 Sheet

192

SPECIAL ISSUES

NAME: In Our Image
DATES LIVED:
NOTED FOR: Bible Character Study With Stamps -
30 Stamps
CLASSIFICATION: Special Issues
SCOTT #: Palau (30) 369 Sheet

NAME: Bible
DATES LIVED:
NOTED FOR: Jerusalem Trimillenum Bible
Characters
CLASSIFICATION: Special Issues
SCOTT #: Palau (30) 396 a-ad - Sheet

NAME: Adam & Eve
DATES LIVED:
NOTED FOR: First Man & Woman
CLASSIFICATION: Special Issues
SCOTT #: Palau 396b

NAME: Noah
DATES LIVED:
NOTED FOR: Famous for Ark
Building Stamps -25
CLASSIFICATION: Special Issues
SCOTT#: Palau 396c

NAME: Abraham
DATES LIVED: 1800BC
NOTED FOR: Prophet, Law Giver
CLASSIFICATION: Special Issues
SCOTT #: Palau 396d

NAME: Jacob
DATES LIVED:
NOTED FOR: Prophet, Law Giver
CLASSIFICATION: Special Issues
SCOTT #: Palau 396e

NAME: Jacob
DATES LIVED:
NOTED FOR: Prophet, Law Giver
CLASSIFICATION: Special Issues
SCOTT #: Palau 396f

NAME: Joseph
DATES LIVED: 1562-1452BC
NOTED FOR: Prophet, Law Giver
CLASSIFICATION: Special Issues
SCOTT #: Palau 396g

NAME: Moses
DATES LIVED: 1391-1271 BC
NOTED FOR: Prophet, Law Giver
CLASSIFICATION: Special Issues
SCOTT #: Palau 396h

NAME: Moses
DATES LIVED: 1391-1271BC
NOTED FOR: Prophet, Law Giver
CLASSIFICATION: Special Issues
SCOTT #: Palau 396i

NAME: Balaam
DATES LIVED:
NOTED FOR: Prophet, Law Giver
CLASSIFICATION: Special Issues
SCOTT #: Palau 396j

NAME: Joshua
DATES LIVED: 1500-1390BC
NOTED FOR: Prophet, Law Giver
CLASSIFICATION: Special Issues
SCOTT #: Palau 396k

NAME: Gideon
DATES LIVED:
NOTED FOR: Prophet, Law Giver
CLASSIFICATION: Special Issues
SCOTT #: Palau 396l

NAME: Jephthah
DATES LIVED:
NOTED FOR: Prophet, Law Giver
CLASSIFICATION: Special Issues
SCOTT #: Palau 396m

NAME: Samson
DATES LIVED:
NOTED FOR: Prophet, Law Giver
CLASSIFICATION: Special Issues
SCOTT #: Palau 396n

NAME: Ruth & Naomi
DATES LIVED:
NOTED FOR: Prophet, Law Giver
CLASSIFICATION: Special Issues
SCOTT #: Palau 396o

NAME: Saul
DATES LIVED:
NOTED FOR: Prophet, Law Giver
CLASSIFICATION: Special Issues
SCOTT #: Palau 396p

NAME: Saul
DATES LIVED:
NOTED FOR: Prophet, Law Giver
CLASSIFICATION: Special Issues
SCOTT #: Palau 396q

NAME: David & Jonathon
DATES LIVED:
NOTED FOR: Prophet, Law Giver
CLASSIFICATION: Special Issues
SCOTT #: Palau 396r

NAME: David & Nathan
DATES LIVED:
NOTED FOR: Prophet, Law Giver
CLASSIFICATION: Special Issues
SCOTT #: Palau 396s

NAME: David
DATES LIVED:
NOTED FOR: Prophet, Law Giver
CLASSIFICATION: Special Issues
SCOTT #: Palau 396t

NAME: Solomon
DATES LIVED: 967BC
NOTED FOR: Prophet, Law Giver
CLASSIFICATION: Special Issues
SCOTT #: Palau 396u

NAME: Solomon
DATES LIVED: 967BC
NOTED FOR: Prophet, Law Giver
CLASSIFICATION: Special Issues
SCOTT #: Palau 396v

SPECIAL ISSUES

NAME: Elijah
DATES LIVED:
NOTED FOR: Prophet, Law Giver
CLASSIFICATION: Special Issues
SCOTT #: Palau 396w

NAME: Elisha
DATES LIVED:
NOTED FOR: Prophet, Law Giver
CLASSIFICATION: Special Issues
SCOTT #: Palau 396x

NAME: Isaiah
DATES LIVED: 800BC
NOTED FOR: Prophet, Law Giver
CLASSIFICATION: Special Issues
SCOTT #: Palau 396z

NAME: Jeremiah
DATES LIVED:
NOTED FOR: Prophet, Law Giver
CLASSIFICATION: Special Issues
SCOTT #: Palau 396aa

NAME: Ezekiel
DATES LIVED: 800BC
NOTED FOR: Prophet, Law Giver
CLASSIFICATION: Special Issues
SCOTT #: Palau 396ab

NAME: Nebuchadnezzar
DATES LIVED: 634-562BC
NOTED FOR: Prophet, Law Giver
CLASSIFICATION: Special Issues
SCOTT #: Palau 396ac

NAME: Amos
DATES LIVED: 750BC
NOTED FOR: Prophet, Law Giver
CLASSIFICATION: Special Issues
SCOTT #: Palau 396ad

SPECIAL ISSUES

NAME: State of Israel
DATES LIVED:
NOTED FOR: 50th Anniversary State of Israel
CLASSIFICATION: Special Issues
SCOTT #: Venezuela 1598 Sheet

SPECIAL ISSUES

NAME: Menorah
DATES LIVED:
NOTED FOR: Menorah
CLASSIFICATION: Special Issues
SCOTT #: Venezuela 1598a

NAME: Moses
DATES LIVED:
NOTED FOR: Moses
CLASSIFICATION: Special Issues
SCOTT #: Venezuela 1598b

NAME: Theodore Herzl
DATES LIVED:
NOTED FOR: Theodore Herzl
CLASSIFICATION: Special Issues
SCOTT #: Venezuela 1598c

NAME: King David
DATES LIVED:
NOTED FOR: King of Israel
CLASSIFICATION: Special Issues
SCOTT #: Venezuela 1598d

NAME: Shofar Blowing
DATES LIVED:
NOTED FOR: Shofar Blowing
CLASSIFICATION: Special Issues
SCOTT #: Venezuela 1598e

NAME: Torah
DATES LIVED:
NOTED FOR: The Torah
CLASSIFICATION: Special Issues
SCOTT #: Venezuela 1598f

NAME: Praying At the Wall
DATES LIVED:
NOTED FOR: Praying at the Wailing Wall
CLASSIFICATION: Special Issues
SCOTT #: Venezuela 1598g

NAME: David Ben-Gurion
DATES LIVED: 1886-1973
NOTED FOR: National Government Leader
CLASSIFICATION: Special Issues
SCOTT #: Venezuela 1598h

NAME: Kinessit
DATES LIVED:
NOTED FOR: Knessit
CLASSIFICATION: Special Issues
SCOTT #: Venezuela 1598i

NAME: Book Museum
DATES LIVED:
NOTED FOR: Book Museum
CLASSIFICATION: Special Issues
SCOTT #: Venezuela 1598j

Ersttagsbrief / First Day Cover
100.Geburtstag Oskar Schindler

Foto: Francesco Pazzi

Deutschland 145

Oskar Schindler 1908-1974
Der Bewahrer eines einzigen Lebens
hat eine ganze Welt bewahrt.

Berlin

Erstausgabe

100. Geburtstag
Oskar Schindler

10117

Herrn
Friedrich Adamo
Karl-Sauer-Str. 7

76829 LANDAU

Deutsche Post ✚

PHILATELIE

„Es wächst ein Baum in Israel,
der sagt, was Mut vermag.
Es wächst ein Baum in Yad Vashem,
der Tragheit tief beschämt.
Es wächst ein Baum in Israel,
der fragt, wer heute hilft."

Dieter Trautwein

OSKAR
SCHINDLER
100.GEBURTSTAG

Foto: pa

Deutschland 145

Oskar Schindler 1908-1974
Der Bewahrer eines einzigen Lebens
hat eine ganze Welt bewahrt.

Berlin 10.04.2008

Erstausgabe

100. Geburtstag
Oskar Schindler

10117

DEUTSCHLAND
exklusiv

NAME: Oskar Schindler
DATES LIVED: 1908-1974
NOTED FOR: Industrialist, Saved Jews from the Holacaust
CLASSIFICATION: Financier, Businessman
SCOTT #: Germany FDC2481

NAME: Oskar Schindler
DATES LIVED: 1908-1974
NOTED FOR: Industrialist, Saved Jews from the Holacaust
CLASSIFICATION: Financier, Businessman
SCOTT #: Germany FDC2481

STATESMEN

STATESMEN

NAME: Leon Blum
DATES LIVED: 1872-1950
NOTED FOR: Statesman
CLASSIFICATION: Statesman
SCOTT #: France 1847

NAME: Rabbi Isaac Herzog
DATES LIVED: 1888-1959
NOTED FOR: Statesman, Scholar
CLASSIFICATION: Statesman
SCOTT #: Israel 892

NAME: Paul Hymans
DATES LIVED: 1965-1941
NOTED FOR: Belgiun Political Statesman
CLASSIFICATION: Statesman
SCOTT #: Belgium 622

NAME: Henry Kissenger
DATES LIVED: 1923-date
NOTED FOR: American Statesman, Politician
CLASSIFICATION: Statesman
SCOTT #: Micronesia 379f

NAME: Ya'acov Meridor
DATES LIVED: 1913-1995
NOTED FOR: Government
CLASSIFICATION: Statesman
SCOTT #: Israel 1518

NAME: Abba Hillel Silver
DATES LIVED: 1893-1963
NOTED FOR: Statesman
CLASSIFICATION: Statesman
SCOTT #: Israel 778

NAME: Joseph Sprinzak
DATES LIVED: 1885-1959
NOTED FOR: Speaker of Kinesset
CLASSIFICATION: Statesman
SCOTT #: Israel 946

STATESMEN

NAME: Willy Brandt
DATES LIVED: 1913-1992
NOTED FOR: German Politician, Statesman,
Chancellor, non-Jewish but friend of Jews,
first Chancellor to visit Israel
CLASSIFICATION: Statesmen
SCOTT #: Antigua & Barbuda 1688

NAME: Leon Blum
DATES LIVED: 1872-1950
NOTED FOR: Statesman
CLASSIFICATION: Statesmen
SCOTT #: France 1847

NAME: Tomas Garrigue Masaryk
DATES LIVED: 1850-1937
NOTED FOR: Lawyer, defender of Zionists and
Jewish rights
CLASSIFICATION: Human Rights
SCOTT #: Czechoslovakia 2772

THEATRICAL DIRECTORS

THEATRICAL DIRECTORS

NAME: Max Reinhardt
DATES LIVED: 1873-1943
NOTED FOR: Theatrical Director
CLASSIFICATION: Theatrical Director
SCOTT #: Austria 952

NAME: Max Reinhardt
DATES LIVED: 1873-1943
NOTED FOR: Theatrical Director
CLASSIFICATION: Theatrical Director
SCOTT #: Germany 1428

UNDERGROUND HEROES

UNDERGROUND HEROES

NAME: Sarah Aaronsohn
DATES LIVED: 1890-1917
NOTED FOR: World War 1 Heroine, Spy
CLASSIFICATION: Underground Hero
SCOTT #: Israel 1076

NAME: Eliyahu Golomb
DATES LIVED: 1893-1945
NOTED FOR: Underground Hero, Founder of
Haganah
CLASSIFICATION: Underground Hero
SCOTT #: Israel 688

NAME: David Raziel
DATES LIVED: 1910-1941
NOTED FOR: British Underground Hero
CLASSIFICATION: Underground Hero
SCOTT #: Israel 690

NAME: Havivah Reik
DATES LIVED: 1914-1944
NOTED FOR: Executed Agent
CLASSIFICATION: Underground Hero
SCOTT #: Israel 994

NAME: Yitzhak Sadeh
DATES LIVED: 1890-1952
NOTED FOR: Underground Hero, Military
CLASSIFICATION: Underground Hero
SCOTT #: Israel 691

NAME: Dr. Moshe Sneh
DATES LIVED: 1909-1972
NOTED FOR: Underground Hero, Military Figure
CLASSIFICATION: Underground Hero
SCOTT #: Israel 689

UNDERGROUND HEROES

NAME: Abraham Stern
DATES LIVED: 1907-1942
NOTED FOR: Underground Heroes
CLASSIFICATION: Underground Hero
SCOTT #: Israel 692

NAME: Adolph Warski
DATES LIVED: 1868-1937
NOTED FOR: Polish Communist Movement
Leader
CLASSIFICATION: Underground Hero
SCOTT #: Poland 2308

NAME: Yitzhak Zuckerman
DATES LIVED: 1915-1981
NOTED FOR: Resistance Hero
CLASSIFICATION: Underground Hero
SCOTT #: Israel 906

NAME: Charlotte Eisenblatter
DATES LIVED: 1903-1944
NOTED FOR: Anti Nazi movement
CLASSIFICATION: Martyrs
SCOTT #: Germany B51

NAME: Pesti Barnabas
DATES LIVED: 1920-1944
NOTED FOR: born Jozsef Getzler, Chemical
Engineer, Underground Hungarian Communist,
father Jewish
CLASSIFICATION: Underground Heroes
SCOTT #: Hungary (1973) 2260

WRITERS

.

NAME: M.J. Berdvczewski
DATES LIVED: 1865-1921
NOTED FOR: Israili Writer
CLASSIFICATION: Writer
SCOTT #: Israel 1269a

NAME: Yehuda Burla
DATES LIVED: 1886-1969
NOTED FOR: 1st Modern Hebrew Writer
CLASSIFICATION: Writer
SCOTT #: Israel 1269b

NAME: Devorah Baron
DATES LIVED: 1887-1920
NOTED FOR: Hebrew Writer
CLASSIFICATION: Writer
SCOTT #: Israel 1269c

NAME: Haim Hazaz
DATES LIVED: 1898-1973
NOTED FOR: Hebrew Writer of Literacy Fiction
CLASSIFICATION: Writer
SCOTT #: Israel 1269d

NAME: Judah Lieb Gordon
DATES LIVED: 1830-1892
NOTED FOR: Hebrew Poet, Writer
CLASSIFICATION: Writer
SCOTT #: Israel 1269e

NAME: Yossef Hayyim Brenner
DATES LIVED: 1881-1921
NOTED FOR: Author of Plays, Short Stories, Novels
CLASSIFICATION: Writer
SCOTT #: Israel 1269f

NAME: Abraham Shlonsky
DATES LIVED: 1900-1973
NOTED FOR: Hebrew Writer, Poet
CLASSIFICATION: Writer
SCOTT #: Israel 1269g

NAME: Yaacov Shabtai
DATES LIVED: 1934-1981
NOTED FOR: Wrote Sketches, Plays, & Novels
CLASSIFICATION: Writer
SCOTT #: Israel 1269h

NAME: Issac Lieb Peretz
DATES LIVED: 1852-1915
NOTED FOR: Yiddish Writer
CLASSIFICATION: Writer
SCOTT #: Israel 1269i

NAME: Nathan Alterman
DATES LIVED: 1910-1970
NOTED FOR: Hebrew Writer, Poet, Playwrite
CLASSIFICATION: Writer
SCOTT #: Israel 1269j

NAME: Shaul Tchernichovsky
DATES LIVED: 1875-1943
NOTED FOR: Poet
CLASSIFICATION: Writer
SCOTT #: Israel 1269k

NAME: Amir Gilboa
DATES LIVED: 1917-1982
NOTED FOR: Hebrew Writer of Poetry
CLASSIFICATION: Writer
SCOTT #: Israel 1269L

NAME: Yokheved Bat Miraim
DATES LIVED: 1901-1980
NOTED FOR: Israli Poet
CLASSIFICATION: Writer
SCOTT #: Israel 1269m

NAME: Mendele Mokher Sefarim
DATES LIVED: 1835-1917

NOTED FOR: Grandfather of Yiddish Literature
CLASSIFICATION: Writer
SCOTT #: Israel 1269n

WRITERS

NAME: Shmuel Yosef Agnon
DATES LIVED: 1880-1970
NOTED FOR: Writer
CLASSIFICATION: Writer
SCOTT #: Israel 776

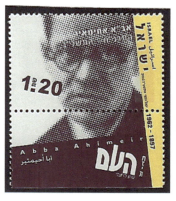

NAME: Abba Ahimeir
DATES LIVED: 1897-1962
NOTED FOR: Political Writer
CLASSIFICATION: Writer
SCOTT #: Israel 1493

NAME: Sholom Alechim
DATES LIVED: 1859-1916
NOTED FOR: Yiddish Writer
CLASSIFICATION: Writer
SCOTT #: Israel 154

NAME: Shalom Alechim
DATES LIVED: 18591916
NOTED FOR: Yiddish Writer
CLASSIFICATION: Writer
SCOTT #: Russia 2164

NAME: Sholom Alechim
DATES LIVED: 1859-1916
NOTED FOR: Yiddish Writer
CLASSIFICATION: Writer
SCOTT #: Romania 1268

NAME: Yehuda Amichai
DATES LIVED: 1924-2000
NOTED FOR: Poet
CLASSIFICATION: Writer
SCOTT #: Israel 1453

NAME: Hannah Arendt
DATES LIVED: 1906-1975
NOTED FOR: German-American Political Theorist
CLASSIFICATION: Writer
SCOTT #: Germany 1489

NAME: Perez Bernstein
DATES LIVED: 1890-1971
NOTED FOR: Writer
CLASSIFICATION: Writer
SCOTT #: Israel 802

WRITERS

NAME: Israel Abihssira
DATES LIVED: 1890-1984
NOTED FOR: Book Writer,
Pen Name of Sidna "Baba Sali"
CLASSIFICATION: Writers
SCOTT #: Israel 1384

NAME: Yitzhak Baer
DATES LIVED: 1888-1980
NOTED FOR: German Historian Writer
CLASSIFICATION: Writer
SCOTT #: Israel 1477

NAME: Moshe Beilinson
DATES LIVED: 1890-1936
NOTED FOR: Political Writer
CLASSIFICATION: Writer
SCOTT #: Israel 1495

NAME: Rabbi Binyamin
DATES LIVED: 1880-1957
NOTED FOR: Political Writer
CLASSIFICATION: Writer
SCOTT #: Israel 1496

NAME: Rachel Blustein
DATES LIVED: 1890-1931
NOTED FOR: Poet
CLASSIFICATION: Writer
SCOTT #: Israel 1077

NAME: Joseph Brodsky
DATES LIVED: 1940-1996
NOTED FOR: Poet and Essayist
CLASSIFICATION: Writer
SCOTT #: Russia 3696

NAME: Joseph Brodsky
DATES LIVED: 1940-1996
NOTED FOR: Poet and Essayist
CLASSIFICATION: Writer
SCOTT #: Nicauragua 2135k

NAME: Albert Camus
DATES LIVED: 1914-1960
NOTED FOR: Writer, Nobel In Literature-1957
CLASSIFICATION: Writer
SCOTT #: Niger 409

WRITERS

NAME: Miguel de Cervantes
DATES LIVED: 1547-1616
NOTED FOR: Spanish Novelist, Poet
CLASSIFICATION: Writer
SCOTT #: Israel 1300

NAME: Benzion Dinur
DATES LIVED: 1884-1973.
NOTED FOR: Historian Writer
CLASSIFICATION: Writer
SCOTT #: Israel 1476

NAME: Simone Dubnow
DATES LIVED: 1860-1941
NOTED FOR: Historian Writer
CLASSIFICATION: Writer
SCOTT #: Israel 1475

NAME: Frederick Dannay
DATES LIVED: 1905-1982
NOTED FOR: Ellery Queen TV & Books
CLASSIFICATION: Writer
SCOTT #: San Marino 949

NAME: Bob Dylan
DATES LIVED: 1941-date
NOTED FOR: American Singer, Writer, Poet
CLASSIFICATION: Writer
SCOTT #: Gambia 1825

NAME: Anne Frank
DATES LIVED: 1929-1945.
NOTED FOR: Victim of Holocaust, Writer of a Diary
CLASSIFICATION: Writer
SCOTT #: Netherlands 598

WRITERS

NAME: (L.L. Zamenhof) Esperanto
DATES LIVED: 1859-1917
NOTED FOR: Created International Auxilliary Language
CLASSIFICATION: Writer
SCOTT #: Poland 859

NAME: (L.L. Zamenhof) Esperanto
DATES LIVED: 1859-1917
NOTED FOR: Created International Auxilliary Language
CLASSIFICATION: Writer
SCOTT #: Cuba 2926

NAME: Anne Frank
DATES LIVED: 1929-1945
NOTED FOR: Victim of Holocaust, Writer of a Diary
CLASSIFICATION: Writer
SCOTT #: Germany 1293

NAME: Egon Friedell
DATES LIVED: 1878-1938
NOTED FOR: Writer, Political Activist, Nobel in Literature
CLASSIFICATION: Writer
SCOTT #: Austria 1072

NAME: Anne Frank
DATES LIVED: 1929-1945
NOTED FOR: Victim of Holocaust, Writer of a Diary
CLASSIFICATION: Writer
SCOTT #: Israel 985

NAME: Leah Goldberg
DATES LIVED: 1911-1970
NOTED FOR: Poet, Playwrite
CLASSIFICATION: Writer
SCOTT #: Israel 1078

WRITERS

NAME: Leah Goldberg
DATES LIVED: 1911-1970
NOTED FOR: Author, "Apartment to Let"
CLASSIFICATION: Writer
SCOTT #: Israel 893

NAME: Heinrich Graetz
DATES LIVED: 1817-1891
NOTED FOR: Historian Writer
CLASSIFICATION: Writer
SCOTT #: Israel 1474

NAME: Uri Zvi Grinberg
DATES LIVED: 1896-1981
NOTED FOR: Poet
CLASSIFICATION: Writer
SCOTT #: Israel 859

NAME: Emile Habiby
DATES LIVED: 1921-1996
NOTED FOR: Journalist
CLASSIFICATION: Writer
SCOTT #: Israel 1544

NAME: Heinrich Heine
DATES LIVED: 1797-1856
NOTED FOR: German Poet
CLASSIFICATION: Writer
SCOTT #: Germany 1098

NAME: Heinrich Heine
DATES LIVED: 1797-1856
NOTED FOR: German Poet
CLASSIFICATION: Writer
SCOTT #: Germany 1984

NAME: Heinrich Heine
DATES LIVED: 1797-1856
NOTED FOR: German Poet
CLASSIFICATION: Writer
SCOTT #: Israel 1460

NAME: Lorenz Hart
DATES LIVED: 1895-1943
NOTED FOR: Songwriter
CLASSIFICATION: Writer
SCOTT #: United States 3347

WRITERS

NAME: Herman Heijermans
DATES LIVED: 1864-1924
NOTED FOR: Dutch Writer
CLASSIFICATION: Writer
SCOTT #: Netherlands B503

NAME: Paul J. Heyse
DATES LIVED: 1830-1914
NOTED FOR: Writer, Nobel Prize in Literature-
1910 - 2 Stamps
CLASSIFICATION: Writer
SCOTT #: Sweden (2) 878

NAME: Oscar Hammerstein II
DATES LIVED: 1895-1960
NOTED FOR: Songwriter
CLASSIFICATION: Writer
SCOTT #: United States 3348

NAME: Karl Kraus
DATES LIVED: 1874-1936
NOTED FOR: Austrian Writer & Journalist
CLASSIFICATION: Writer
SCOTT #: Austria 986

NAME: Franz Kafka
DATES LIVED: 1883-1924
NOTED FOR: Writer
CLASSIFICATION: Writer
SCOTT #: Czechoslavakia 1633

NAME: Alan Jay Lerner
DATES LIVED: 1918-1986
NOTED FOR: Songwriter
CLASSIFICATION: Writer
SCOTT #: United States 2770

NAME: Alan Jay Lerner
DATES LIVED: 1918-1986
NOTED FOR: Songwriter
CLASSIFICATION: Writer
SCOTT #: United States 3346

WRITERS

NAME: Fritz Lang
DATES LIVED: 1890-1976
NOTED FOR: Austrian Filmmaker, Screenwriter
CLASSIFICATION: Writer
SCOTT #: Dominica 944 M/S

NAME: Frank Loesser
DATES LIVED: 1910-1969
NOTED FOR: Songwriter
CLASSIFICATION: Writer
SCOTT #: United States 3350

NAME: Primo Levi
DATES LIVED: 1919-1987
NOTED FOR: Chemist, Writer, Holocaust Survivor
CLASSIFICATION: Writer
SCOTT #: Italy 3158

NAME: Abraham Mapu
DATES LIVED: 1808-1867
NOTED FOR: Novelist, Historian
CLASSIFICATION: Writer
SCOTT #: Israel 376

WRITERS

NAME: Georges Mandel
DATES LIVED: 1885-1944
NOTED FOR: French Political Journalist
CLASSIFICATION: Writer
SCOTT #: France 1104 Imperf

NAME: Marcel Proust
DATES LIVED: 1871-1922
NOTED FOR: French Novelist, Critic
CLASSIFICATION: Writer
SCOTT #: France B396

NAME: Georges Mandel
DATES LIVED: 1885-1944
NOTED FOR: French Political Journalist
CLASSIFICATION: Writer
SCOTT #: France 1104 Perf.

NAME: Emanuel Ringelblum
DATES LIVED: 1900-1944
NOTED FOR: Historian Writer
CLASSIFICATION: Writer
SCOTT #: Israel 1553

NAME: Ayn Rand
DATES LIVED: 1905-82
NOTED FOR: Writer
CLASSIFICATION: Writer
SCOTT #: United States 3308

NAME: Richard Rodgers
DATES LIVED: 1902-1979
NOTED FOR: Songwriter
CLASSIFICATION: Writer
SCOTT #: United States 3348

WRITERS

NAME: Nellie Sachs
DATES LIVED: 1891-1970
NOTED FOR: German Literature, Playwrite
CLASSIFICATION: Writer
SCOTT #: Germany 1695

NAME: Nellie Sacks
DATES LIVED: 1891-1970
NOTED FOR: German Literature, Playwrite
CLASSIFICATION: Writer
SCOTT #: Sweden 2399b

NAME: Avraham Schlonsky
DATES LIVED: 1900-1973
NOTED FOR: Hebrew Writer, Poet
CLASSIFICATION: Writer
SCOTT #: Israel 1319 M/S

NAME: Arthur Schnitzer
DATES LIVED: 1862-1931
NOTED FOR: Austrian Author and Dramatist
CLASSIFICATION: Writer
SCOTT #: Austria 1396

WRITERS

NAME: Dimetrie Cantemir
DATES LIVED: 1673-1723
NOTED FOR: Notated Musivcal Pieces, Writer
CLASSIFICATION: Writer
SCOTT #: Russia 4132

NAME: Jacob Talmon
DATES LIVED: 1916-1980
NOTED FOR: Historian Writer
CLASSIFICATION: Writer
SCOTT #: Israel 1554

NAME: Kurt Tucholsky
DATES LIVED: 1890-1935
NOTED FOR: German Journalist, Satirist, Writer
CLASSIFICATION: Writer
SCOTT #: Germany 9N506

NAME: Franz Werfel
DATES LIVED: 1890-1945
NOTED FOR: Czech Writer
CLASSIFICATION: Writer
SCOTT #: Austria 1516

NAME: Franz Werfel
DATES LIVED: 1890-1945
NOTED FOR: Czech Writer
CLASSIFICATION: Writer
SCOTT #: Deutchland Germany 1904

NAME: Eliezer Ben-Yehuda
DATES LIVED: 1858-1922
NOTED FOR: Lexicographer & Editor
CLASSIFICATION: Writer
SCOTT #: Israel 156

NAME: Stefan Zweig
DATES LIVED: 1881-1942
NOTED FOR: Austrian Novelist, Playwrite
CLASSIFICATION: Writer
SCOTT #: Austria 1199

WRITERS

NAME: Egon Erwin Kisch
DATES LIVED: 1885-1948
NOTED FOR: Czech Writer, Journalist
CLASSIFICATION: Writers
SCOTT #: East Germany 2651

NAME: Moses Rashi
DATES LIVED: 1040-1105
NOTED FOR: Scholar and Bible Interpreter,
Schlomo Yitzchaki
CLASSIFICATION: Writer
SCOTT #: Israel 1012

NAME: Else Lasker Schuler
DATES LIVED: 1869-1945
NOTED FOR: Writer, Short Stories, Novelist,
Playwright
CLASSIFICATION: Writer
SCOTT #: Germany 1155

NAME: Joseph Pulitzer
DATES LIVED: 1847-1947
NOTED FOR: Hungarian Newspaper Publisher,
Journalist, Prize Named After Him
CLASSIFICATION: Writers
SCOTT #: United States 946

NAME: St. Therese of Avila
DATES LIVED: 1515-1582
NOTED FOR: Jewish grandmother, Author, Spanish
Mystic
CLASSIFICATION: Writers
SCOTT #: France 1846

WRITERS

ПАШТОЎКА

адрас адпраўнічыка і індэкс прадпрыемства сувязі

Абразкі

1886-1941
Змітрок БЯДУЛЯ

БЕЛАРУСЬ BELARUS 2011

B

Каму

Куды

індэкс

Аповесці Казкі Апавяданні

Міністэрства сувязі і інфарматызацыі Рэспублікі Беларусь
РУП «БЕЛПОШТА» 2011 г www.belpost.by Мастак М Рыжы
РУП «Брэсцкая ўзбуйненая друкарня им А Ц Непагодзіна
Зак 588ц 2011 Тыр 30000 Код 303-11

NAME: Zmitrok Biadulia
DATES LIVED: 1886-1941
NOTED FOR: Russian, pen name of Shmuel Plaunik,
Poetry
CLASSIFICATION: Writers
SCOTT #: Belarus Postcard 1101

NAME: Sigfried Sassoon
DATES LIVED: 1886-1967
NOTED FOR: English Poet, Writer,m Soldier
CLASSIFICATION: Writer
SCOTT #: St. Helena 971

NAME: Sidney Sheldon
DATES LIVED: 1917-2007
NOTED FOR: American Writer, Playwright, Producer
CLASSIFICATION: Writers
SCOTT #: Guyana 3453

WRITERS

NAME: Georg Brandes
DATES LIVED: 1842-1927
NOTED FOR: Danish Physicist- Nobel Prize in 1922
CLASSIFICATION: Scientist
SCOTT #: Denmark 486

NAME: Robert Jungk
DATES LIVED: 1872-1937
NOTED FOR: Austrian writer (Robert Baum)
CLASSIFICATION: Writers
SCOTT #: Austria 2444

NAME: Emile Zola
DATES LIVED: 1840-1902
NOTED FOR: French novelist, playwright
CLASSIFICATION: Writers
SCOTT #: Czechoslovakia 2774

NAME: Hugo L. Hoffmanstahl
DATES LIVED: 1874-1929
NOTED FOR: Austrian Birth Centenary, Jewish born
Grandfather, Poet
CLASSIFICATION: Writers
SCOTT #: Austria 980

NAME: Ivan Olbracht
DATES LIVED: 1882-1952
NOTED FOR: born Kamil Zeman, Novelist, Czech
writer
CLASSIFICATION: Writers
SCOTT #: Czechoslovakia 781

NAME: Eva Cox
DATES LIVED: 1938-present
NOTED FOR: Austrian born Writer, Sociologist,
Activist
CLASSIFICATION: Writers
SCOTT #: Australia 3404

WRITERS

NAME: Egon Friedell
DATES LIVED: 1878-1938
NOTED FOR: Actor, Philosopher
CLASSIFICATION: Philosophers
SCOTT #: Austria 1072

NAME: Jacob Daniel du Toit
DATES LIVED: 1877-1953
NOTED FOR: Bible Translator, So. African poet,
Scholar
CLASSIFICATION: Writers
SCOTT #: South Africa 473

NAME: Samuel Marshak
DATES LIVED: 1887-1964
NOTED FOR: Russian Author, Poet, Translator
CLASSIFICATION: Writers
SCOTT #: Russia 5612

NAME: Moss Hart
DATES LIVED: 1904-1961
NOTED FOR: American Broadway Playwrite,
Director
CLASSIFICATION: Writers
SCOTT #: United States 3882

NAME: Moses Rashi
DATES LIVED: 1040-1105
NOTED FOR: Scholar and Bible Interpreter,
Schlomo Yitzchaki
CLASSIFICATION: Writer
SCOTT #: France 3088

NAME: Carl Zuckmeyer
DATES LIVED: 1896-1977
NOTED FOR: German writer, Playwright
CLASSIFICATION: Writers
SCOTT #: Germany 1950

WRITERS

NAME: Danilo Kis
DATES LIVED: 1935-1989
NOTED FOR: Yugoslav Writer and Novelist
CLASSIFICATION: Writers
SCOTT #: Montenegro 241

NAME: Egon Erwin Kisch
DATES LIVED: 1885-1948
NOTED FOR: Czech Writer, Journalist
CLASSIFICATION: Writers
SCOTT #: Germany 1439

NAME: Kurt Tucholsky
DATES LIVED: 1890-1935
NOTED FOR: German Journalist, Satirist, Writer
CLASSIFICATION: Writer
SCOTT #: Germany 9N506

NAME: Pricilla Denise Levertoff
DATES LIVED: 1923-1997
NOTED FOR: Poet, Book writer
CLASSIFICATION: Writers
SCOTT #: United States 4661

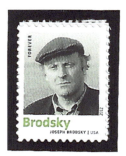

NAME: Joseph Brodsky
DATES LIVED: 1940-1996
NOTED FOR: Russian-Americam Poet, Essayist,
Nobel Winner 1987
CLASSIFICATION: Writers
SCOTT #: United States 4654

NAME: Julian Tuwim
DATES LIVED: 1894-1953
NOTED FOR: Lyricist, Poet, Polish- Pseudonym,
"Olden"
CLASSIFICATION: Writers
SCOTT #: Poland 1714

WRITERS

NAME: Barbara Frum
DATES LIVED: 1937-1992
NOTED FOR: American born, Canadian famous TV

Journalist

CLASSIFICATION: Writers
SCOTT #: Canada 1821 a-d

NAME: Jorge Isaacs
DATES LIVED: 1837-1895
NOTED FOR: Author, Columbian Romantic movement
CLASSIFICATION: Writers
SCOTT #: Columbia 971

NAME: Paul Claudel
DATES LIVED: 1868-1955
NOTED FOR: Non Jewish, Published many favorable

writings for Jews

CLASSIFICATION: Writers
SCOTT #: France B420

ZIONISTS

ZIONISTS

NAME: Rabbi Yehuda Hai Alkalai
DATES LIVED: 1798-1878
NOTED FOR: Zionist
CLASSIFICATION: Zionist
SCOTT #: Israel 1029

NAME: Israel Eldad
DATES LIVED: 1910-1996
NOTED FOR: Political Writer - Zionist
CLASSIFICATION: Zionist
SCOTT #: Israel 1494

NAME: Michael Halperin
DATES LIVED: 1860-1919
NOTED FOR: Zionist
CLASSIFICATION: Zionist
SCOTT #: Israel 857

NAME: Theodore Herzl
DATES LIVED: 1860-1904
NOTED FOR: Zionist Founder
CLASSIFICATION: Zionist
SCOTT #: Israel 86

NAME: Theodore Zeev Herzl
DATES LIVED: 1860-1904
NOTED FOR: Zionist Founder
CLASSIFICATION: Zionist
SCOTT #: Israel 51

NAME: Theodore Herzl
DATES LIVED: 1860-1904
NOTED FOR: Zionist Founder
CLASSIFICATION: Zionist
SCOTT #: Israel 183

NAME: Theodore Herzl
DATES LIVED: 1860-1904
NOTED FOR: Zionist Founder
CLASSIFICATION: Zionist
SCOTT #: Israel 1566

NAME: Theodore Herzl
DATES LIVED: 1860-1904
NOTED FOR: Zionist Founder
CLASSIFICATION: Zionist
SCOTT #: Israel 695

ZIONISTS

NAME: Theodore Herzl
DATES LIVED: 1860-1904
NOTED FOR: Zionist Founder
CLASSIFICATION: Zionist
SCOTT #: Israel 1699

NAME: Ze'ev Jabotinsky
DATES LIVED: 1880-1940
NOTED FOR: Writer, Zionist Leader
CLASSIFICATION: Zionist
SCOTT #: Israel 409a

NAME: Ze'ev Jabotinsky
DATES LIVED: 1880-1940
NOTED FOR: Writer, Zionist Leader
CLASSIFICATION: Zionist
SCOTT #: Israel 1071

NAME: Ze'ev Jabotinsky
DATES LIVED: 1880-1940
NOTED FOR: Writer, Zionist Leader
CLASSIFICATION: Zionist
SCOTT #: Israel 706

NAME: Charles Netter
DATES LIVED: 1826-1882
NOTED FOR: College Founder, Zionist Leader
CLASSIFICATION: Zionist
SCOTT #: Israel 417

NAME: Berl Katzenelson
DATES LIVED: 1887-1944
NOTED FOR: Leader of Labor Zionist Org.
CLASSIFICATION: Zionist
SCOTT #: Israel 713

ZIONISTS

NAME: Max Nordau
DATES LIVED: 1849-1923
NOTED FOR: Hungarian Zionist Leader,
Physician, Author
CLASSIFICATION: Zionist
SCOTT #: Israel 780

NAME: Leon Pinsker
DATES LIVED: 1821-1891
NOTED FOR: Hovevei Zion Founder
CLASSIFICATION: Zionist
SCOTT #: Israel 880

NAME: Baron Edmond Rothschild
DATES LIVED: 1845-1934
NOTED FOR: French Zionist, Banker
CLASSIFICATION: Zionist
SCOTT #: Israel 90

NAME: Arthur Ruppin
DATES LIVED: 1876-1943
NOTED FOR: Zionist Hero & Leader
CLASSIFICATION: Zionist
SCOTT #: Israel 740

NAME: Henrietta Szold
DATES LIVED: 1860-1945
NOTED FOR: Founder of Hadassah Womens
Org., Zionist
CLASSIFICATION: Zionist
SCOTT #: Israel 188

NAME: Menachem Ussishkin
DATES LIVED: 1863-1941
NOTED FOR: Head of Jewish National Fund
CLASSIFICATION: Zionist
SCOTT #: Israel 712

THIS PAGE LEFT BLANK ON PURPOSE

NOTED SPREADSHEETS FOR STAMPS

LAST NAME	FIRST NAME	DATES LIVED	FIELD OF KNOWLEDGE	HERO CLASSIFICATION	COUNTRY OF STAMP	SCOTT # OF STAMP
Aaronsohn	Aaron	1876-1919	Botanist, Agronomist	Scientists	Israel	742
Aaronsohn	Sarah	1890-1917	World War 1 Heroine, Spy	Underground Heroes	Israel	1076
Abbott	Bud	1895-1974	Comedian, Actor Producer	Actors, Entertainers	Gambia	1348d
Abbott	Bud	1895-1974	Comedian, Actor Producer	Actors, Entertainers	United States	2566
Abhissira	Israel	1890-1984	Book Writer - Pen Name of Sidna	Actors, Entertainers	Israel	1384
Abraham		1800BC	Prophet, Law Giver	Special Issues	Palau	396d
Adam & Eve			First Man & Woman	Special Issues	Palau	396b
Adler	Jankel	1895-1949	Printmaker, Painter - "The Purim Players"	Artists, Painters	Israel	568
Adler	Viktor	1852-1918	Austrian Politician, SDAP founder	Politicians	Austria	1094
Adler	Saul	1895-1966	Scientist	Scientists	Israel	1202
Adler	Victor	1852-1918	Socialist, Politician	Socialist	Austria	1094
Agam	Yaacov	1928-date	Painter, Artist, Designer - "Independence Day"	Artists, Painters	Israel	838
Agnon	Samuel	1888-1970	Writer, Nobel Prize in Literature	Writers	Antigua	1945a
Agnon	Samuel	1888-1970	Writer, Nobel Prize in Literature	Writers	Antigua	1945a
Agnon	Shmuel Yosef	1880-1970	Writer	Writers	Isreal	776
Ahlmeir	Abba	1897-1962	Political Writer	Writers	Israel	1493
Alechim	Sholom	1859-1916	Yiddish Writer	Writers	Israel	154
Alechim	Sholom	1859-1916	Yiddish Writer	Writers	Romania	1268
Alechim	Shalom	1859-1916	Yiddish Writer	Writers	Russia	2164
Alkachi	Mordechai	1925-1947	Martyr	Martyrs	Israel	831i
Alkalal	Rabbi Yehuda Hai	1798-1878	Zionist	Zionists	Israel	1029
Allen	Gracia	1895-1964	American Comedian	Actors, Entertainers	Grenada	2554
Allen	Gracia	1895-1964	American Actor, teamed with George Burns	Actors, Entertainers	United States	4414P
Alion	Yigdal	1918-1980	Military	Military	Isreal	858
Aloni	Nissim	1928-1988	Theatre	Actors, Entertainers	Israel	1627
Alpari	Gyula	1882-1944	Hungarian Communist Politician	Politicians	Germany	898
Alpari	Gyula	1882-1944	Hungarian Communist Politician	Politicians	Hungary	3420
Alterman	Nathan	1910-1970	Hebrew Writer, Poet, Playwrite	Writers	Israel	1269j
Altman	Sidney	1939-present	Canadian-American molecular biolooist	Scientists	Antigua & Barbuda	2518D
Amichai	Yehuda	1924-2000	Poet	Writers	Israel	1453
Amiel	Moshe Avigdor	1883-1945	Rabbi	Rabbis	Israel	969
Amos		750BC	Prophet, Law Giver	Special Issues	Palau	396ad
Andrei	Bernath	1908-1944	Victim of Nazi Terrorism	Human Rights	Romania	B265
Anielewicz	Mordechai	1919-1943	WW2 Uprising Leader	Martyrs	Israel	841c S/S
Antokololsky	Mark	1843-1902	Russian Sculptor	Artists, Painters	Russia	1993 Post Card
Ardon	Mordechai	1896-1992	Abstractionist, Painter - "Jerusalem Painting"	Artists, Painters	Israel	773
Ardon	Mordechai	1896-1992	Stained Glass Artist	Artists, Painters	Israel (2)	1041 S/S
Arendt	Hannah	1906-1975	German-American Political Theorist	Writers	Germany	1489
Argov	Zohar	1914-1995	Musician	Musicians	Israel	1773A
Argov	Sasha	1955-1987	Musician	Musicians	Israel	1773B
Arlel	Meir	1942-1999	Musician	Musicians	Israel	1773C
Aroff	Chana	1888-1968	Ukranian Artist, Sculptor	Artists, Painters	Israel	538
Arndt	Rudi	1909-1940	Musician, Artist,	Musicians	Germany	636
Aron	Raymond	1905-1983	French Philosopher Sociologist, Journalist	Philosophers	France	3152
Aron	Raymond	1905-1983	French Philosopher, Professor	Philosophers	France	3837
Ascher	Leo	1880-1942	Composer of Operettas	Composers , Musicians	Austria	1160
Ascher	Leo	1880-1942	Composer of Operettas	Composers , Musicians	Austria	1280
Asser	Tobias	1838-1913	1911 Nobel Prize in Peace, Legal Scholar	Educator, Scholar	Netherlands	800
Asser	Tobias	1836-1913	Statesman & Jurist, Legal Scholar	Statesmen	Netherlands	800
Aumann	Robert	1930-date	Economics Nobel Prize - 2005	Scientists	St Thomas & Prince Islands	2143 Sheet
Auschwitz Berkenau			German Concentration Camp		DCR	2294
Avila	St Therese of	1515B-1582	Jewish Grandmother, Author, Spanish Mystic	Other	France	1846
Azaar	Samuel	1929-1955	Martyr For Independence	Martyrs	Israel	831Q
Azulai	Rabbi Hayyim Joseph ben	1724-1806	Rabbi	Rabbis	Israel	1110
Ba'al	Rabbi Meir	139-163	Jewish Sage Scholar	Educator Scholar	Israel	731
Bacall	Lauren	1924-date	Film and Stage Actress	Actors, Entertainers	Grenada Grenadines	1778h
Bacall	Lauren	1924-2014	(Betty Joan Perske) - Actress, Singer, Movie Star	Actors, Entertainers	Senegal	1425F
Bach	Johann	1685-1750	German Composer, Violinist	Composers, Musicians	Israel	1408
Baeck	Leo	1873-1956	German Rabbi, Scholar, Theologian –	Rabbis	Germany	777
Baer	Yitzhak	1888-1980	German Historian Writer	Writers	Israel	1477
Balaam			Prophet, Law Giver	Spacial Issues	Palau	396j
Ballin	Albert	1857-1918	German shipping magnate	Financiers, Businessmen	Germany	769
Banal	Yossi	1932-2006	Musician	Musicians	Israel	1773D
Banki	Donat	1859-1922	Hungarian Engineer, co-invented Carburetor	Inventors	Hungary	4128
Bara	Theda	1885-1955	Movie Star - Silent Screen	Actors, Entertainers	United States	2827

LAST NAME	FIRST NAME	DATES LIVED	FIELD OF KNOWLEDGE	HERO CLASSIFICATION	COUNTRY OF STAMP	SCOTT # OF STAMP
Barany	Robert	1876-1936	Austrian-Hungarian Otologist, Nobel in Philosophy, Medicine	Scientists	Austria	1031
Barany	Robert	1876-1936	Austrian-Hungarian Otologist, Nobel in Philosophy, Medicine	Scientists	Chad	719
Barany	Robert	1876-1936	Austrian-Hungarian Otologist, Nobel in Philosophy, Medicine	Scientists	Hungary	3155
Barany	Robert	1876-1936	Austrian-Hungarian Otologist, Nobel In Philosophy, Medicine	Scientists	Sweden	1105
Barazani	Moshe	1921-1947	Martyr For Independence	Martyrs	Israel	831O
Bard	Ida Holz	1935-present	Engineering and Computer Science Professor	Scientists	Uruguay	2529
Bar-Ilan	Rabbi Meir	1880-1949	Rabbi, Founder of Movement	Rabbis	Israel	855
Barnabas	Pestl	1920-1944	born Jozsef Getzler, Chemical Engineer, Underground Hungarian Communist, father Jewish	Underground Heroes	Hungary (1973)	2260
Barnard	Dr. Christian	1922-2001	So. African 1st. Heart Transplant, Physician	Scientists	Dominica	2001
Baron	Devorah	1887-1920	Hebrew Writer	Writers	Dominica	1269c
Basri	Yosef	1923-1952	Martyr For Independence	Martyrs	Israel	831T
Bat Miraim	Yokheved	1901-1980	srail Poet	Writers	Israel	1269m
Bauer	Otto	1881-1938	Austrian Social Democrat	Socialist	Austria	1186
Bayer	Adolph Von	1835-	German Chemist-Nobel Prize In 1905	Scientists	Sweden	689
Begin	Menachim	1913-1992	Prime Minister	National Government Leaders	Dominica	1207D
Begin	Menachim	1913-1992	Prime Minister	National Government Leaders	Israel	1153
Begin	Menachim	1913-1992	Prime Minister	National Government Leaders	Israel	1551
Begin	Menachim	1913-1992	Prime Minister	National Government Leaders	Israel (9)	1551 SHEET
Bellinson	Moshe	1890-1936	Political Writer	Writers	Israel	1495
Beit	Sir Alfred	1853-1906	British gold and diamond magnate	Financiers, Businessmen	Rhodesia	262
Belkind	Naaman	1889-1917	Martyr For Independence	Martyrs	Israel	831E
Ben Yossi	Schlomo	1913-1938	First Jew in Gallows of Palestine	Martyrs	Israel	831C
Benatzky	Ralph	1884-1957	Composer of the "White Horse Inn"	Composers ,Musicians	Austria	1280
Benenson	Peter	1927-2005	English Lawyer-Founder of Human Rights Amnesty International	Human Rights	Denmark	790
Benenson	Peter	1927-2005	English Lawyer-Founder of Human Rights Amnesty International	Human Rights	Micronesia	379l
Ben-Gurion	David	1886-1973	Prime Minister of Israel	National Government Leaders	Israel	547
Ben-Gurion	David	1886-1973	Prime Minister of Israel	National Government Leaders	Israel	548
Ben-Gurion	David	1886-1973	Prime Minister of Israel	National Government Leaders	Israel	705
Ben-Gurion	David ben	1886-1973	Government	National Government Leaders	Israel	950
Ben-Gurion	David	1886-1973	Prime Minister of Israel	National Government Leaders	Israel (13)	1572 Sheet
Ben-Gurion	David	1886-1973	National Government Leader	Special Issues	Venezuela	1598h
Benny	Jack	1894-1979	Comedian	Actors, Entertainers	Grenada	2084
Benny	Jack	1894-1979	Comedian	Actors, Entertainers	United States	2564
Benny	Jack	1894-1974	Singer, Actor, Comedian	Comedians	Grenada	2550
Ben-Yehuda	Eliezer	1858-1922	Lexicographer & Editor	Writers	Israel	156
Ben-Zvi	Itzhak	1884-1963	President of Israel	National Government Leaders	Israel	255
Ben-Zvi	Rachel Yanait	1886-1979	President of Israel	National Government Leaders	Israel	1096
Berdvczewski	M.J.	1865-1921	Israli Writer	Writers	Israel	1269a
Berg	Gertrude	1899-1966	Radio & Television Actress	Actors, Entertainers	Grenada	2551
Berger	Isaac	1936-present	Israeli born American Weightlifter, won 2 Olympic Silvers	Athletes	Dominica	2040C
Berger	Isaac	1936-present	Israli-American Weight Lifter, 2 Olympic Medals	Athletes	Dominica	Mi 2465
Berger	Michel	1947-1992	Singer	Musicians	France	2823
Bergson	Henri	1859-1941	French Philosopher	Philosophers	France	934
Berlin	Irving	1888-1989	American Composer	Composers ,Musicians	United States	3669
Bernhardt	Sarah	1844-1923	French Stage Actress	Actors, Entertainers	Antigua	1567
Bernhardt	Sarah	1844-1923	French Stage Actress	Actors, Entertainers	France	B191
Bernhardt	Sarah	1844-1923	French Stage Actress	Actors, Entertainers	Monaco	1931
Bernhardt	Sarah	1844-1923	French Stage Actress	Actors, Entertainers	Monaco	1981
Bernstein	Leonard	1918-1990	American Musician, Conductor	Musicians	Gambia	2050e
Bernstein	Leonard	1918-1990	American Musician, Conductor	Musicians	Gambia	2050f
Bernstein	Leonard	1918-1990	American Musician, Conductor	Musicians	Gambia	2050g
Bernstein	Leonard	1918-1990	American Musician, Conductor	Musicians	Gambia	2050g
Bernstein	Leonard	1918-1990	American Musician, Conductor	Musicians	Gambia	2050h
Bernstein	Leonard	1918-1990	American Musician, Conductor	Musicians	Israel	1226
Bernstein	Perez	1890-1971	Writer	Writers	United States	3521
Bet-Tzuri	Eliyahu	1922-1945	Martyr For Independence	Martyrs	Israel	802
Bladulia	Zmitrok	1886-1941	Russian, pen name of Shmuel Plaunik, Poetry	Writers	Israel	831A
Bialik	Chaim Nachman	1873-1934	Artist	Artists, Painters	Belarus	Postcard 1101
Bialik	Chaim Nachman	1873-1934	Artist	Artists, Painters	Israel	155
Bible			Jerusalem Trmillenum Bible Characters	Special Issues	Israel	895
Bingen	Jaques	1908-1944	French Underground Resistance	Educator, Scholar	Palau (30)	396 a-ad - Sheet
Binyamin	Rabbi	1880-1957	Political Writer	Writers	France	882
Blankinship	Cecil Stuart	1904-1973	Architect, 'Habitat Stamp UN Conference' designer	Artists, Painters	Israel	1496
					Canada	690

LAST NAME	FIRST NAME	DATES LIVED	FIELD OF KNOWLEDGE	HERO CLASSIFICATION	COUNTRY OF STAMP	SCOTT # OF STAMP
Bloch	Ernest	1880-1959	Composer	Composers, Musicians	Israel	1225
Bloch	Felix	1905-1983	Swiss Physicist	Scientists	Guyana	3008f
Blum	Rene	1889-1967	Politician, Diplomat	Politicians	Monaco	636
Blum	Leon	1872-1950	Statesman	Statesmen	France	1847
Blum	Leon	1872-1950	Statesman	Statesmen	Israel	1330e
Blumberg	Baruch	1925-2011	Physician, Nobel in Prize in Psysiology-1976	Scientists	Maldives	2113e
Blustein	Rachel	1890-1931	Poet	Writers	Israel	1077
Bohr	Neils	1885-1962	Danish Physicist- Nobel Prize in 1922	Scientists	Denmark	409
Bohr	Neils	1885-1962	Danish Physicist- Nobel Prize in 1922	Scientists	Denmark	409 A Phosphorus
Bohr	Neils	1885-1962	Danish Physicist- Nobel Prize in 1922	Scientists	Denmark	410 Phosphorus
Bohr	Neils	1885-1962	Danish Physicist- Nobel Prize in 1922	Scientists	Denmark	410A
Bohr	Neils	1885-1962	Danish Physicist- Nobel Prize in 1922	Scientists	Malagasy	1132a
Bohr	Neils	1885-1962	Danish Physicist- Nobel Prize in 1922	Scientists	Maldives	2116a
Bolaffi	Alberto (brother Aste)	1874-1944	World renowned Philatelist, Publisher	Financiers, Businessmen	Antigua & Barbuda	1667
Book Museum			Book Museum	Special Issues	Venezuela	1598j
Borge	Victor	1909-2000	born Borge Rosenbaum, Entertainer, Pianist	Actors, Entertainers	Denmark	1394
Born	Max	1882-1970	Physicist,Quantum Theory, Nobel Prize	Scientists	Germany	1381
Born	Max	1882-1970	German Physicist & Mathematician	Scientists	Malagasy	1132b
Born	Max	1882-1970	German Physicist & Mathematician	Scientists	Malagasy	1132b
Brandeis	Louis D.	1856-1941	Supreme Court Justice from Prague, Legal Scholar	National Government Leaders	United States	4422 C S/S
Brandeis	Georg	1842-1927	Writer, Literary Critic, Scholar	Writers	Denmark	486
Brandes	Georg	1842-1927	Danish Physicist- Nobel Prize in 1922	Scientists	Denmark	486
Brandt	Willy	1913-1992	German Politician, Statesman, Chancellor	Statesmen	Antigua & Barbuda	1688
Brenner	Yossef Hayyim	1881-1921	Author of Plays, Short Stories, Novels	Writers	Israel	1269f
Brice	Fanny	1891-1951	Comedian, Singer	Actors, Entertainers	United States	2565
Brodsky	Joseph	1940-1996	Poet and Essayist	Writers	Nicaragua	2135k
Brodsky	Joseph	1940-1996	Poet and Essayist	Writers	Russia	3696
Brodsky	Joseph	1940-1996	Russian-Americam Poet, Essayist, Nobel Winner 1987	Writers	United States	4654
Brown	Joe E.	1892-1973	Vaudville Singer, Actor	Actors, Entertainers	Gambia	1993
Brown	Joe E.	1892-1973	Vaudville Singer, Actor	Actors, Entertainers	Grenada	2087
Brown	Joe E.	1891-1973	American Films, Movies, Walk of Fame	Actors, Entertainers	St. Vincent	1562t-h
Brunschvicg	Cecile	1877-1946	Born CecileKahn, French Feminist Politician	Politicians	France	6478
Buber	Martin	1878-1965	Philosopher	Philosophers	Germany	1268
Buber	Martin	1878-1965	Philosopher	Philosophers	Israel	1362f
Burla	Yehuda	1886-1969	1st Modern Hebrew Writer	Writers	Israel	1269b
Burns	George	1896-1996	American Actor, Comedian, Writer	Actors, Entertainers	Grenada	2554
Burns	George	1896-1996	American Actor	Actors, Entertainers	United States	4414P
Caly	Odette	1914-1993	French Artist, "La Corbeille Rose"	Artists, Painters	France	Mi 2473
Camus	Albert	1914-1960	Writer, Nobel In Literature-1957	Writers	Niger	409
Canada-Israel		2010	60 years of Relations, 1st Day Cover	Other	Canada	2379
Canetti	Elias	1905-1994	Bulgarian Novelist, Playwrite	Writers	Maldives	2116d
Cantemir	Dimetrie	1673-1723	Notated Musivcal Pieces, Writer	Writers	Russia	4132
Cantor	Eddie	1892-1964	Comedian, Singer, Actor	Actors, Entertainers	Grenada	2552
Cassin	Rene	1887-1976	Nobel Prize of 1968 for Human Rights	Human Rights	France	2689
Cassin	Rene	1887-1976	Nobel Prize of 1968 for Human Rights	Human Rights	Malagasy	943
Cassin	Rene	1887-1976	Nobel Prize of 1968 for Human Rights	Human Rights	Malagasy	943
Castillo	Jose A.	1920 Flight	Equador Aviation pioneer, Owner "El Telegrapho'	Inventors	Equador	283
Castillo	Jose A.	1920 Flight	Equador Aviation pioneer, Owner "El Telegrapho'	Inventors	Equador	285
Castillo	Jose A.	1920 Flight	Equador Aviation pioneer, Owner "El Telegrapho'	Inventors	Equador	C282
Castillo	Jose A.	1920 Flight	Equador Aviation pioneer, Owner "El Telegrapho'	Inventors	Equador	284
Castillo	Jose A.	1920 Flight	Equador Aviation pioneer, Owner "El Telegrapho'	Inventors	Equador	594
Castillo	Jose A.	1920 Flight	Equador Aviation pioneer, Owner "El Telegrapho'	Inventors	Equador	595
Cervantes	Miguel de	1547-1616	Spanish Novelist, Poet	Writers	Israel	1300
Chagall	Marc	1887-1985	Russian Painter	Artists, Painters	Israel	399
Chagall	Marc	1887-1985	Russian Painter	Artists, Painters	Monaco	1599
Chalfie	Martin	1947-date	Chemistry Nobel Prize - 2008	Scientists	St. Thomas & Prince Islands	2143 Sheet
Choral Synagogue			Lithuania Synagogue in Vilnus, Still used	Other	Lithuania	New 2017 Issue (ENV)
Christ	Jesus	0 AD-32AD	Born Jewish	Martyrs	Nicaragua (3)	971-73
Claudel	Paul	1868-1955	Non-Jewish, Published many favorable writings-for Jews	Writers	France	B420
Cogan	Moise (Moshe)	1879-1943	Illustrator, Sculptor, Graphic Artist, died in Aoschwitz	Artists, Painters	Moldova	4
Cohen	Eli	1924-1965	Martyr For Independence	Martyrs	Israel	831P
Copland	Aaron	1900-1990	American Classical Composer	Musicians	Grenada Grenadines	1865g
Copperfield	David	1956-present	born David Seth Kotkin, Illusionist, Magician	Magicians	Dominica	2241
Copperfield	David	1956-date	Magician, Illusionist	Magicians	Grenada Grenadines	2239
Copperfield	David	1956-date	Magician, Illusionist	Magicians	Grenada Grenadines	2239

LAST NAME	FIRST NAME	DATES LIVED	FIELD OF KNOWLEDGE	HERO CLASSIFICATION	COUNTRY OF STAMP	SCOTT # OF STAMP
Copperfield	David	1956-present	born David Seth Kotkin, Illusionist, Magician	Magicians	Nevis	1229
Cox	Eva	1938-present	Austrian born Writer, Sociologist, Activist	Writers	Australia	3404
Crying Eye		1937-1945	Symbol	Other	St. Thomas & Prince Islands	2245 Sheet
Cukor	George	1899-1983	American Film Director	Film	Hungary	3668
Cupped Hands		1937-1945	Symbol	Other	St. Thomas & Prince Islands	2245 Sheet
Damari	Shoshana	1923-2006	Musician	Musicians	Israel	1773F
Danial			Danial and the Lion - Sheet	Special Issues	Guyana	2836
Danial & The Lion			Bible Story on Stamps - 25 Stamps	Special Issues	Guyana (25)	2836
Dannay	Frederick	1905-1982	Ellery Queen Book Fictional Character	Writers	San Marino	949
Dassault	Marcel	1892-1986	French Aircraft Industrialist	Financier, Businessman	France	2085
David			King of Israel	National Government Leaders	Israel	185
David			Prophet, Law Giver	Special Issues	Palau	396t
David	King		King of Israel	Special Issues	Venezuela	1598d
David & Goliath		1010Bc	Bible Story David Slays GoliathWith Stamps - 25	Special Issues	Guyana (25)	2651 Sheet
David & Jonathon			Prophet, Law Giver	Special Issues	Palau	396r
David & Nathan			Prophet, Law Giver	Special Issues	Palau	396s
Davis, Jr.	Sammy	1925-1990	Singer, Converted to Judiasm, Entertainer, Dancer	Actors, Entertainers	Malagasy Republic	1055
Dayan	Moshe	1915-1981	Minister of Defense	National Government Leaders	Israel	1000
De Castro	Morris Fidanque	1902-1966	First US Virgin Islands Governor	National Government Leaders	Cuba	390
de Mille	Agnes	1905-1993	American Dancer & Choreographer, Journalist	Journalists	United States	3842
Debre	Michel Jean Pierre	1912-1996	1st Prime Minister of France	National Government Leaders	France	2622
Destinn	Emmy	1878-1920	Czech Singer, Actor	Actors, Entertainers	Czechoslovakia	624
Di Torres	Luis Baez di	?-1493	born Josef benLevi, converted to Catholicism, Interpretor of Columbus	Contribution to World Culture	Cuba	390
Di Torres	Luis Baez di	?-1493	born Josef benLevi, converted to Catholicism, Interpretor of Columbus	Contribution to World Culture	Norfolk Islands	560A
Dinur	Benzion	1884-1973	Historian Writer	Writers	Israel	1476
Disraeli	Benjamin	1804-1881	British Prime Minister	National Government Leaders	Great Britain	1190
Dizengoff	Meir	1861-1936	Mayor of Tel Aviv, Founder	National Government Leaders	Israel	919
Djerassi	Carl	1923-2015	Bulgarian World Reknowned Chemist, Oral Contraceptive	Scientists	Austria	1990
Dori	Ya'acov	1899-1973	Israeli Defense	Military	Israel	1519
Douglas	Kirk	1916-date	Actor, Filmstar	Actors, Entertainers	Grenada (6)	2136-41 'Sheet
Douglas	Kirk	1916-date	Actor, Filmstar	Actors, Entertainers	Mali	693
Douglas	Melvyn	1901-1981	father Jewish, American Actor	Actors, Entertainers	Senegal	1425C
Douglas	Kirk	1916-date	Actor, Filmstar	Actors, Entertainers	Sierre Leone	1993
Douglas	Michael	1944-present	UN Messenger of Peace, movie star, actor, producer	Statesmen	Sierra Leone	2846A-B
Dovatar	Lev	-1942	Cossack General killed	Military	Russia	862
Dresner	Yechiel	1922-1947	Martyr For Independence	Martyrs	Israel	831G
du Toit	Jacob Daniel	1877-1953	Bible Translator, So. African poet, Scholar	Writers	South Africa	473
Dubinsky	David	1892-1982	American Labor Leader	Other	Maldives	1161
Dubnow	Simone	1860-1941	Historian Writer	Writers	Israel	1475
Duca	Ion G.	1879-1933	Victim of Nazi Terrorism, Prime Minister of Romania	National Government Leaders	Romania	B261
Dukas	Paul	1865-1935	French Composer	Musicians	France	B389
Dumont	Santos	1873-1932	Brazilian who Sponsored Flight Around Eiffel Tower Aviator,	Financiers, Businessmen	Brazil	713-14
Durer	Albrecht	1441-1528	Artist, Painter	Artists, Painters	Chad	373 S/S
Durer	Albrecht	1471-1528	German Painter, Engraver	Artists, Painters	Paraguay	1804
Durkheim	Emile	1858-1917	French Sociologist	Sociologists	Israel	1362a
Dylan	Bob	1941-date	American Singer, Writer, Poet	Writers	Gambia	1825
Eban	Abba	1915-2002	Government	National Government Leaders	Israel	1652
Ehrlich	Paul	1854-1915	Medical Fief of Blood Work	Immunologist	Germany	1362b
Ehrlich	Paul	1854-1932	American Biologist & Educator	Scientists	Germany	722
Ehrlich	Paul	1879-1955	American Biologist & Educator	Scientists	Sweden	805 Hor. Coil
Ehrlich	Paul	1854-1932	American Biologist & Educator	Scientists	Sweden	805 Vert. Coil
Ehrlich	Paul	1854-1932	American Biologist & Educator	Scientists	Sweden (2)	805 Booklet
Einstein	Albert	1879-1955	Physicist, Mathematician	Scientists	Austria	1960
Einstein	Albert	1879-1955	Physicist, Mathematician	Scientists	Bosnia Herzegovina	401
Einstein	Albert	1879-1955	Physicist, Mathematician	Scientists	Chad	718
Einstein	Albert	1879-1955	Physicist, Mathematician	Scientists	Comoro Islands	207
Einstein	Albert	1879-1955	Physicist, Mathematician	Scientists	France	3112
Einstein	Albert	1879-1955	Physicist, Mathematician	Scientists	France	1299
Einstein	Albert	1879-1955	Physicist, Mathematician	Scientists	Ghana	2192
Einstein	Albert	1879-1955	Physicist, Mathematician	Scientists	Israel	117
Einstein	Albert	1879-1955	Physicist, Mathematician	Scientists	Israel	1609
Einstein	Albert	1879-1955	Physicist, Mathematician	Scientists	Israel	1620
Einstein	Albert	1879-1955	Physicist, Mathematician	Scientists	Israel	1620
Einstein	Albert	1879-1955	Physicist, Mathematician	Scientists	Israel	1220d
Einstein	Albert	1879-1955	Physicist, Mathematician	Scientists	Israel	1220d

LAST NAME	FIRST NAME	DATES LIVED	FIELD OF KNOWLEDGE	HERO CLASSIFICATION	COUNTRY OF STAMP	SCOTT # OF STAMP
Einstein	Albert	1879-1955	Physicist, Mathematician	Scientists	Israel	1330d
Einstein	Albert	1879-1955	Physicist, Mathematician	Scientists	Italy	2048
Einstein	Albert	1879-1955	Physicist, Mathematician	Scientists	Malagasy	1132a
Einstein	Albert	1879-1955	Physicist, Mathematician	Scientists	Malagasy	1132a
Einstein	Albert	1879-1955	Physicist, Mathematician	Scientists	Marshall Islands	627i
Einstein	Albert	1879-1955	Physicist, Mathematician	Scientists	Mexico	C592
Einstein	Albert	1879-1955	Physicist, Mathematician	Scientists	Monaco	2311
Einstein	Albert	1879-1955	Physicist, Mathematician	Scientists	Monaco	2371
Einstein	Albert	1879-1955	Physicist, Mathematician	Scientists	Mongolia (9)	2451-59 S/S
Einstein	Albert	1879-1955	Physicist, Mathematician	Scientists	New Guinea	2137
Einstein	Albert	1879-1955	Physicist, Mathematician	Scientists	New Guinea	2137
Einstein	Albert	1879-1955	Physicist, Mathematician	Scientists	Paraguay	875
Einstein	Albert	1879-1955	Physicist, Mathematician	Scientists	Paraguay	877
Einstein	Albert	1879-1955	Physicist, Mathematician	Scientists	Russia	4741
Einstein	Albert	1879-1955	Physicist, Mathematician	Scientists	San Marino	947
Einstein	Albert	1879-1955	Physicist, Mathematician	Scientists	Sierre Leone	1847 S/S
Einstein	Albert	1879-1955	Physicist, Mathematician	Scientists	Swaziland	438
Einstein	Albert	1879-1955	Physicist, Mathematician	Scientists	Sweden	1387
Einstein	Albert	1879-1955	Physicist, Mathematician	Scientists	Togo	1021
Einstein	Albert	1879-1955	Physicist, Mathematician	Scientists	Togo	1022
Einstein	Albert	1879-1955	Physicist, Mathematician	Scientists	Togo	382-3 S/S
Einstein	Albert	1879-1955	Physicist, Mathematician	Scientists	Togo	C381
Einstein	Albert	1879-1955	Physicist, Mathematician	Scientists	Togo	C382
Einstein	Albert	1879-1955	Physicist, Mathematician	Scientists	Togo	C383
Einstein	Albert	1879-1955	Physicist, Mathematician	Scientists	Togo	C384
Einstein	Albert	1879-1955	Physicist, Mathematician	Scientists	Togo (2)	C380 S/S
Einstein	Albert	1879-1955	Physicist, Mathematician	Scientists	United States	1285
Einstein	Albert	1879-1956	Physicist, Mathematician	Scientists	United States	1774
Einstein	Albert	1879-1955	Physicist, Mathematician	Scientists	United States	1774
Eisenblatter	Charlotte	1903-1944	Anti Nazi movement	Martyrs	Germany	B51
Eisler	Gerhard	1897-1968	German politician, father Jewish, Communist	Politicians	Germany	1854
Eisner	Kurt	1867-1919	Politician, Bayern Prime Minister, Murdered in Munich	National Government Leaders	Bayern	Sch 193
Eldad	Israel	1910-1996	Political Writer - Zionist	Zionists	Israel	1494
Eliachar	Jacob Saul	1817-1906	Rabbi	Rabbis	Israel	1646
Elijah	Rabbi Hayyim Joseph ben	1834-1909	Rabbi	Rabbis	Israel	1111
Elijah		800BC	Prophet, Law Giver	Special Issues	Palau	396w
Elisha			Prophet	Prophets	Palau	396
Elisha		800BC	Prophet, Law Giver	Special Issues	Palau	396x
Elsa	Dutchess	1874-1938	Dutchess of Liechtenstein-married to Franz Joseph	Special Issues	Lietchenstein	92
Ensor	James	1860-1949	Belgium Painter	National Government Leaders	Israel	1365a
Erhlich	Paul	1854-1915	American-German Scientist, Hemotology	Artists, Painters	Gambia	909
Erhlich	Paul	1854-1915	American-German Scientist, Hemotology	Scientists	Gambia	909
Erhlich	Paul	1854-1915	American-German Scientist, Hemotology	Scientists	Gambia	909
Erhlich	Paul	1854-1915	American-German Scientist, Hemotology	Scientists	Sweden	805
Erhlich	Paul	1854-1915	American-German Scientist, Hemotology	Scientists	Sweden	807
Eshkol	Levi	1895-1969	Prime Minister of Israel	Scientists	Israel	408
Esperanto	(L. L. Zamenhof)	1859-1917	Created International Auxilliary Language	National Government Leaders	Brazil	1761
Esperanto	(L. L. Zamenhof)	1859-1917	Created International Auxilliary Language	Writers	Cuba	2926
Esperanto	(L. L. Zamenhof)	1859-1917	Created International Auxilliary Language	Writers	Poland	859
Ezekiel		800BC	Prophet, Law Giver	Writers	Israel	525
Ezekiel			Prophet	Prophets	Palau	398ab
Fairbanks	Douglas	1883-1939	Actor	Special Issues	United States	2088
Fall	Leo	1873-1925	Austrian Composer of Operettas	Actors, Entertainers	Austria	1021
Felix	Elizabeth Rachel	1821-1858	Activist	Composers , Musicians	Israel	1330f
Feynman	Richard	1918-1988	Theoretical Physicist - Quantum Mechanics	Human Rights	United States	3909
Fielder	Arthur	1894-1979	Musician, Boston Pops	Scientists	United States	3159
Finder	Pawel	1904-1944	Polish-Jewish Communist Leader- 1st Sec. of Polish Workers Party	Musicians	Poland	2532
Fine	Larry	1902-1975	Movie and Television Actor- Three Stooges	National Government Leaders	Senegal	1433-34
Finestein	Meir	1927-1947	Martyr For Independence	Actors, Entertainers	Israel	831N
Fire	Andrew	1959-date	Physiology Nobel Prize - 2006	Martyrs	St. Thomas & Prince Islands	2143 Sheet
Fischer	Bobby	1943-2008	American World Chess Champion	Scientists	Iceland	442
Fischer	Annie	1898-1964	Hungarian Pianist	Chess Masters	Hungary	4308, Mi 5687
Fizikus (Szilard)	Leo	1898-1964	Physicist, Atomic Reactors	Composers , Musicians	Hungary	3592
Flag of Israel		1948	State of Israel Flag	Scientists	Israel	15
Florence (Ferenc)	Rozsa	1906-1942	Journalist	Other	Hungary	B181
				Journalists		

235

LAST NAME	FIRST NAME	DATES LIVED	FIELD OF KNOWLEDGE	HERO CLASSIFICATION	COUNTRY OF STAMP	SCOTT # OF STAMP
France	Pierre Mendes	1907-1982	French Politician, Pres. Of Council of Ministry	Politicians	France	1906
Franck	James	1882-1964	mother Jewish, Physicist, Nobel winner	Scientists	Germany	1381
Frank	Anne	1929-1945	Victim of Holocaust, Writer of a Diary	Writers	Germany	1293
Frank	Anne	1929-1945	Victim of Holocaust, Writer of a Diary	Writers	Israel	985
Frank	Anne	1929-1945	Victim of Holocaust, Writer of a Diary	Writers	Netherlands	598
Frankel	Leo	1844-1896	Hungarian Socialist	Socialogist	Hungary	938
Frankfurter	Felix	1882-1965	Supreme Court Justice, Legal Scholar	National Government Leaders	United States	4422 A S/S
Freid	Alfred	1864-1921	Austrian Publicist, Nobel Prize, Psychoanalsis Founders	Scientists	Austria	1484
Freud	Sigmund	1856-1939	Psychoanalysis Founder	Psychoanalists	Austria	1175
Freud	Sigmund	1856-1939	Psychoanalysis Founder	Psychoanalists	Grenada	510
Freud	Sigmund	1856-1939	Psychoanalysis Founder	Psychoanalists	Israel	1362e
Freud	Sigmund	1856-1939	Psychoanalysis Founder	Psychoanalists	Mali	345
Freud	Sigmund	1856-1939	Psychoanalysis Founder	Psychoanalists	Marshall Islands	627e
Freud	Sigmund	1856-1939	Psychoanalysis Founder	Psychoanalists	Mexico	2038
Friedell	Egon	1878-1938	Actor, Philosopher	Philosophers	Austria	1072
Friedell	Egon	1878-1938	Writer, Political Activist, Nobel in Literature	Writers	Austria	1072
Frum	Barbara	1937-1992	American born, Canadian famous TV Journalist	Writers	Canada	1821 a-d M/S (D)
Fuerst	Gandor	1903-1932	Communist Party Official	National Government Leaders	Hungary	B179
Gainsbourg (Goldberg)	Serge (Lucien)	1928-1991	French Singer, pianist, song writer	Composers , Musicians	France	2821
Gambetta	Leon	1838-1882	Lawyer, Prime Minister of France	National Government Leaders	France	Mi 378
Garland	Judy	1922-1969	American Actress, Singer	Actors, Entertainers	Antigua	1043
Gershwin	George	1898-1937	American Musician, Composer, Pianist	Musicians	Grenada Grenadines	1865C
Gershwin	George	1898-1937	American Musician, Composer, Pianist	Musicians	Israel	1330b
Gershwin	George	1898-1937	American Musician, Composer, Pianist	Musicians	Malagasy	873
Gershwin	George	1898-1937	American Musician, Composer, Pianist	Musicians	Monaco	2092
Gershwin	George	1898-1937	American Musician, Composer, Pianist	Musicians	St. Vincent	1144
Gershwin	George	1898-1937	American Musician, Composer, Pianist	Musicians	St. Vincent	1144
Gershwin	George	1898-1937	American Musician, Composer, Pianist	Musicians	United States	1484
Gershwin	Ira	1896-1983	American Lyricist, Songwriter	Musicians	United States	3345
Gershwin	George	1898-1937	American Musician, Composer, Pianist	Musicians	United States	3345
Gerstl	Richard	1883-1908	Austrian painter& draughtsman	Artists, Painters	Austria	2453
Gideon			Prophet, Law Giver	Special Issues	Palau	396i
Giehse	Therese	1898-1975	German Actress, born Therese Gift	Actors, Entertainers	Germany	1484
Gilboa	Amir	1917-1982	Hebrew Writer of Poetry	Writers	Israel	1269L
Glazman	Yosef	1908-1943	WW2 Uprissing Leader	Martyrs	Israel (2)	841A S/S
Glicksberg	Haim	1904-1970	Painter, Artist - "Street In Jerusalem"	Artists, Painters	Israel	682
Goldberg	Leah	1911-1970	Author, "Apartment to Let"	Writers	Israel	893
Goldberg	Leah	1911-1970	Poet, Playwrite	Writers	Israel	1078
Goldfaden	Avram	1840-1908	Businessman, 1st Yiddush Theater	Financier, Businessman	Romania	5142A
Goldmark	Karl	1830-1915	Hungarian Composer	Composers , Musicians	Hungary	C133
Golomb	Eliyahu	1893-1945	Underground Hero, Founder of Haganah	Underground Heroes	Israel	688
Gompers	Samuel	1850-1924	AFL-CIO Labor Union Leader	Labor Leaders	United States	988
Goode	Alexander David	1911-1943	Rabbi Chaplain in US Army, Military	Military	United States	956
Goodman	Benny	1909-1986	Jazz & Swing Musician	Musicians	Dominica	1861
Goodman	Benny	1909-1986	Jazz & Swing Musician	Musicians	St. Vincent	1144
Goodman	Benny	1909-1986	Jazz & Swing Musician	Musicians	United States	3099
Gordimer	Nadine	1923-date	Writer, Political Activist, Nobel in Literature	Writers	Antigua	1945b
Gordimer	Nadine	1923-date	Writer, Political Activist, Nobel in Literature	Writers	Antigua	1945b
Gordon	Aharon David	1856-1922	Laborer	Labor Leaders	Israel	1543
Gordon	Judah Lieb	1830-1892	Hebrew Poet, Writer	Writers	Israel	1269e
Gottchaik	Louis	1829-1869	Musician, Composer, Pianist	Musicians	United States	3165
Gottlieb	Maurycy	1856-1879	Printmaker, Painter - "Yom Kippur"	Artists, Painters	Israel	569
Gracia	Donna	1510-1569	Philanthropist	Financiers, Businessmen	Israel	1097
Graetz	Heinrich	1817-1891	Historian Writer	Writers	Israel	1474
Greene	Lorne	1915-1987	Canadian Star of Bonanza, Actor	Actors, Entertainers	Canada	2153A-D
Gregoire	Abbe	1750-1831	Established Civil Rights for Jews in Francein 1791	Human Rights	France	2232B
Grinberg	Uri Zvi	1896-1981	Poet	Writers	Israel	869
Gruenbaum	Yitzhak	1879-1970	Minister of Interior	National Government Leaders	Israel	754
Gruner	Dov	1912-1947	Martyr For Independence	Martyrs	Israel	831H
Gruner	Dov	1912-1947	Israeli Sculptor, Zionist	Zionists	Czechoslavakia	1478
Guber	Rikvah	1902-1981	Educator	Educator, Scholar	Israel	1103
Guigui	Albert	1944-present	Chief Rabbi of Brussels, 1st Rabbi on Belgian stamp	Rabbis	Belgium	2802
Gutenberg	Johannes	1398-1468	Inventor of the Printing Press	Inventors	United States	1014
Gutenberg			Printed Bible	Writers	Germany	723
Haam	Ahad	1856-1927	Composer	Composers , Musicians	Israel	1290

LAST NAME	FIRST NAME	DATES LIVED	FIELD OF KNOWLEDGE	HERO CLASSIFICATION	COUNTRY OF STAMP	SCOTT # OF STAMP
Haber	Fritz	1868-1934	German Chemist, Nobel Recipient 1918	Scientists	Sweden	1271
Haberman	Bronislaw	1882-1947	Czech. Musician, Violinist	Musicians	Israel	954
Habiby	Emile	1921-1996	Journalist	Writers	Israel	1544
Haffkin	Waldemar Mordecai	1860-1930	Bacteriologist, Discovered Cholera Syrum	Scientists	India	387
Haffkine	Mordechai	1860-1930	Developed Cholera Vaccine	Scientists	Israel	1196
Hakham	Rabbi Shimon	1843-1910	Rabbi who Promoted Literacy	Rabbis	Israel	1087
Hakim	Eliahu	1925-1945	Martyr For Independence	Martyrs	Israel	831J
Halevy	Moshe	1895-1974	Theatre	Actors, Entertainers	Israel	1625
Halperin	Michael	1860-1919	Zionist	Zionists	Israel	857
Haman	Esther	400BC	Revealed to a King she was Jewish	Human Rights	Russia	4516
Hamburger	Jeno	1883-1936	Hungarian Politician, People's Commissar of Agriculture	Politicians	Hungary	2784
Hammerstein II	Oscar	1895-1960	Songwriter	Writers	United States	3348
Hananya	Yehoshua ben	1864-1945	Rabbi, Sage, Zionist	Rabbis	Israel	730
Hankin	Yehoshua	1865-1945	Land Developer	Financier, Businessman	Israel	1545
Hannah			Biblical Woman	Other	Israel	885
Harburg	E.Y. "Yipsel"	1896-1981	Born IsidoreHochberg, Lyricist and Songwriter	Composers , Musicians	United States	3905
Hart	Lorenz	1895-1943	Songwriter	Writers	United States	3347
Hart	Moss	1904-1961	American Broadway Playwrite, Director	Writers	United States	3882
Hassan	Sir Joshua	1915-1997	Gibraltan Politician	Politicians	Gibraltar	745
Haviv	Avasholom	1926-1947	Martyr For Independence	Martyrs	Israel	831L
Haza	Ofra	1957-2000	Musician	Musicians	Israel	1773L
Hazaz	Haim	1898-1973	Hebrew Writer of Literacy Fiction	Writers	Israel	1269d
Head	Edith	1897-1981	American Famous Movie Costume Designer, Artist	Film	United States	3772C
Heart & Barbed Wire		1937-1945	Symbol	Other	St. Thomas & Prince Islands	2245 Sheet
Heijermans	Herman	1864-1924	Dutch Writer	Writers	Netherlands	B503
Heine	Heinrich	1797-1856	German Poet, Writer	Writers	Germany	740
Heine	Heinrich	1797-1856	German Poet	Writers	Germany	1098
Heine	Heinrich	1797-1856	German Poet	Writers	Germany	1984
Heine	Heinrich	1797-1856	German Poet	Writers	Israel	1460
Hepburn	Katherine	1907-2003	American Actress- of Jewish descent, Sewell Hepbron	Actors, Entertainers	Grenada Grenadines	1778g
Hepburn	Katherine	1907-2003	American Actress- of Jewish descent, Sewell Hepbron	Actors, Entertainers	Senegal	1425B
Hermann	Bernard	1911-1975	Musician	Musicians	United States	3341
Hertz	Heinrich	1857-1894	Grandfather Jewish, Physicist	Scientists	Germany	354
Herzl	Theodore	1860-1904	Theodore Herzl	Special Issues	Venezuela	1598c
Herzl	Theodore Zeev	1860-1904	Zionist Founder	Zionists	Austria	1960
Herzl	Theodore Zeev	1860-1904	Zionist Founder	Zionists	Israel	51
Herzl	Theodore	1860-1904	Zionist Founder	Zionists	Israel	86
Herzl	Theodore	1860-1904	Zionist Founder	Zionists	Israel	183
Herzl	Theodore	1860-1904	Zionist Founder	Zionists	Israel	695
Herzl	Theodore	1860-1904	Zionist Founder	Zionists	Israel	1566
Herzl	Theodore	1860-1904	Zionist Founder	Zionists	Israel	1699
Herzl	Theodore	1860-1904	Promulgator of Zionism	Zionists	St. Thomas & Prince Islands	2140 Sheet
Herzog	Jacob	1921-1972	Ambassador to Canada, Rabbi	National Government Leaders	Israel	555
Herzog	Chaim	1918-1997	President of Israel	National Government Leaders	Israel	1329
Herzog	Rabbi Isaac	1888-1959	Statesman, Scholar	Statesmen	Israel	892
Heschel	Abraham	1907-1972	American Rabbi	Rabbis	Micronesia	370
Heyse	Paul J.	1830-1914	Writer, Nobel Prize in Literature-1910	Writers	Grenada	2490g
Heyse	Paul J.	1830-1914	Writer, Nobel Prize in Literature-1910 - 2 Stamps	Writers	Sweden (2)	878
Hillel	Omer	1926-date	Artist	Artists, Painters	Israel	894
Hirsch	Baron Maurice de	1831-1896	Founder of Jewish Colonization	Other	Israel	1093
Hirsch	Jeanne	1910-2000	UNESCO Director of Philosophy, Swiss Exec. Council Representative	Philosophers	Switzerland	2159
Hitman	Uzi	1952-2004	Musician	Musicians	Israel	1773K
Hoffmanstahl	Hugo L.	1874-1929	Austrian Birth Centenary, Jewish born Grandfather, Poet	Writers	Austria	980
Holocaust Emblem		1937-1944	Amnesty International Design	Other	Denmark	790
Holocaust Memorial				Other	Uruguay	1590
Holtzberg	Simcha	1924-1994	Holocaust Survivor	Holocaust Survivor	Israel	1365
Houdini	Harry	1874-1926	American Magician, Illusionist	Magicians	United States	3651
Howard	Moe	1897-1975	Movie and Television Actor- Three Stooges	Actors, Entertainers	Senegal	1433-34
Howard	Shrimp	1895-1955	Movie and Television Actor- Three Stooges	Actors, Entertainers	Senegal	1433-34
Hudson	Rock	1925-1985	(Ray Harold Scherer) American Film & TV Star	Actors, Entertainers	Antigua	1045
Huldah			Biblical Woman	Other	Israel	887
Hudai	Ron	1944-date	Mayor of Tel Aviv	National Government Leaders	St. Thomas & Prince Islands	2140 Sheet
Hymans	Paul L.	1865-1941	Belgian politician, Liberal Party	Financiers, Businessmen	France	2208
Hymans	Paul L.	1865-1941	Belgian politician, Liberal Party	National Government Leaders	Belgium	622
Hymans	Paul L.	1865-1941	Belgian politician, Liberal Party, Foreign Minister	Politicians	Belgium	619

LAST NAME	FIRST NAME	DATES LIVED	FIELD OF KNOWLEDGE	HERO CLASSIFICATION	COUNTRY OF STAMP	SCOTT # OF STAMP
Hymans	Paul	1965-1941	Belgiun Political Statesman	Statesmen	Belgium	622
Hymans	Max	1900-1961	French Politian and Businessman	Financiers, Businessmen	France	2208
Illes	Monus (Brandstein)	1888-1944	Party Leader, Politician	Politicians	Hungary	3118
In Our Image			Bible Character Study With Stamps - 30 Stamps	Special Issues	Palau (30)	369 Sheet
Isaacs	Jorge	1837-1895	Author, Columbian Romantic movement	Writers	Columbia	971
Isaiah	Michaelangelo Buonarroti	1475-1564	Artist	Artists, Painters	Vatican City	388
Isaiah			Prophet	Prophets	Israel	527
Isaiah		800BC	Prophet, Law Giver	Special Issues	Palau	396z
Iscovescu	Barbo	1818-1854	Romanian painter, Revolutionary movement	Artists, Painters	Romania	2353
Israel Art		Current	Landscape of Jerusalem	Other	Grenada	M/S
Israel Art		Current	Landscape of Jerusalem	Other	Grenada	M/S
Israel Artifacts		1000BC	Art Values - Jewish Relics	Other	Israel	323-28
Israel-Portugal			Joint Issue - Maritime Research with Israel	Other	Portugal	2017 issue
Israels	Josef (Jozef)	1824-1911	Dutch painter	Artists, Painters		
Jabotinsky	Ze'ev	1880-1940	Writer, Zionist Leader	Zionists	Israel	706
Jabotinsky	Ze'ev	1880-1940	Writer, Zionist Leader	Zionists	Israel	1071
Jabotinsky	Ze'ev	1880-1940	Writer, Zionist Leader	Zionists	Israel	409a
Jacob			Prophet, Law Giver	Special Issues	Palau	396e
Jacob			Prophet, Law Giver	Special Issues	Palau	396f
Jacobs	Aletta	1854-1929	First Woman Admitted to a University	Educator, Scholar	Netherlands	591
James	Harry	1916-1983	American Musician, Band Leader in Swing Era	Musicians	Dominica	1863
James	Harry	1916-1983	American Musician, Band Leader in Swing Era	Musicians	St. Vincent	1144
James	Harry	1916-1983	American Musician, Band Leader in Swing Era	Musicians	St. Vincent	1144
Jephthah			Prophet, Law Giver	Special Issues	Palau	396m
Jeremiah			Prophet	Prophets	Israel	526
Jeremiah		655BC	Prophet & Writer	Prophets	Vatican City	390
Jeremiah			Prophet, Law Giver	Special Issues	Palau	396aa
Jewish Relics		1593	Torah Curtain Detail	Other	Czechoslavakia	1475
Jewish Relics		1530	Prague's Printer Emblem	Other	Czechoslavakia	1476
Jewish Relics		1804	Mikulev Jug	Other	Czechoslavakia	1477
Jewish Relics		1939-1945	Memorial for Concentration Camp Victims	Other	Czechoslavakia	1478
Jewish Relics			Pincas Synagogue	Other	Czechoslavakia	1479
Jewish Relics		1613	Tombstone of David Gans	Other	Czechoslavakia	1480
Jewish Relics			Bronze Panther Figurine	Other	Israel	323
Jewish Relics			Synagogue Stone Menorah	Other	Israel	324
Jewish Relics			Phoenician Ivory Sphinx	Other	Israel	325
Jewish Relics			Gold Earring	Other	Israel	326
Jewish Relics			Miniature Gold Capital	Other	Israel	327
Jewish Relics			Gold Drinking Horn	Other	Israel	328
Joachim	Josech	1831-1907	Hungarian Composer, Violinist	Composers , Musicians	Germany	9N280
Job		1562-1452BC	Prophet, Law Giver	Special Issues	Palau	3964
Joel		1600-1100 BC	Prophet in Bible, Statue on Stamp	Prophets	Brazil	872
Joffe	Abraham	1880-1960	Russian Scientist, Chemist	Scientists	Russia	4870
Johanan	Rabbi	200-279	Rabbi, Sandal Maker	Rabbis	Israel	732
Jonah & Whale			Jonah & The Whale Story with Stamps - 25 Stamps	Special Issues	Palau (25)	321 S/S
Jorga	Nikolai	1871-1940	Victim of Nazi Terrorism, Democratic Nationalist Party	National Government Leaders	Romania	B263
Joselewicz	Berek	1764-1809	Colonel of the Polish Army	Military	Israel	1772 S/S
Josen	Al	1886-1950	Singer, Theater, Movies	Actors, Entertainers	Israel	1253
Josen	Al	1886-1950	Singer, Theater, Movies	Actors, Entertainers	Mali	C536
Josen	Al	1886-1950	Singer, Theater, Movies	Actors, Entertainers	Tanzania	1480
Josen	Al	1886-1950	Singer, Theater, Movies	Actors, Entertainers	United States	2849
Josen	Al	1886-1950	Singer, Theater, Movies	Film	Israel	1253
Joseph		1562-1452BC	Prophet, Law Giver	Special Issues	Palau	396g
Joseph 1st.	Franz	1830-1918	King of Hungary,1867	National Government Leaders	Austria	130
Joseph 1st.	Franz	1830-1916	King of Hungary, 1867	National Government Leaders	Austria	150
Joseph 2nd.	Franz	1906-1989	Longest serving Prince of Lietchtenstein	National Government Leaders	Liechtenstein	185
Joseph 2nd.	Franz	1906-1989	Longest serving Prince of Lietchtenstein	National Government Leaders	Liechtenstein	213
Joseph 2nd.	Franz	1906-1989	Longest serving Prince of Lietchtenstein, with wife	National Government Leaders	Liechtenstein	410
Joseph 2nd.	Franz	1906-1989	Longest serving Prince of Lietchtenstein	National Government Leaders	Liechtenstein	710A
Joseph 2nd.	Franz	1906-1989	Longest serving Prince of Lietchtenstein	National Government Leaders	Liechtenstein	710B
Joseph 2nd.	Franz	1906-1989	Longest serving Prince of Lietchtenstein	National Government Leaders	Liechtenstein	710C
Joshua		1500-1390BC	Prophet, Law Giver	Special Issues	Palau	396k
Jungk	Robert	1872-1937	Austrian writer (Robert Baum)	Writers	Austria	2444
Kaduri	Itzhak	1902-2006	Rabbi	Rabbis	Israel	1702
Kafka	Franz	1883-1924	Writer	Writers	Czechoslavakia	1633

LAST NAME	FIRST NAME	DATES LIVED	FIELD OF KNOWLEDGE	HERO CLASSIFICATION	COUNTRY OF STAMP	SCOTT # OF STAMP
Kafka	Franz	1883-1924	Writer	Writers	Israel	1330a
Kahana	Aharon	1905-1967	Sculptor, Painter, Artist - "Resurrection"	Artists, Painters	Israel	483
Kahlo	Frida	1907-1954	German Jewish Father, Mexican Artist, married Diego Kahlo	Artists, Painters	Mexico	2228
Kaiser	Jacob	1888-1961	German Politician, Resistance Fighter	Politicians	Germany	1545
Kaiser	Jacob	1888-1961	German Politician & Resistance Leader in WW2	Politicians	Germany	2226
Kalischer	Hirsch	1795-1874	Rabbi	Rabbis	Israel	1743
Kalman	Emmerich	1882-1953	Hungarian Composer	Composers , Musicians	Austria	1226
Kalman	Emmerich	1882-1953	Hungarian Composer of Operettas	Composers , Musicians	Austria	1226
Kaplin (Kaplan)	David (Viktor)	1876-1934	Austria Engineer, Inventor of Kaplan turbine	Inventors	Austria	B151
Karpov	Antoloy	1951-date	Chess Master	Chess Masters	Cambodia	1556
Karpov	Antoloy	1951-date	Chess Master	Chess Masters	Grenada	3385 S/S
Kashani	Eliezer	1923-1947	Martyr For Independence	Martyrs	Israel	831F
Kasparov	Garry	1963-date	Chess Master	Chess Masters	Cambodia	1557 M/S
Katchalsky-Katzir	Aharon	1913-1972	Chemist	Scientists	Israel	1166
Kato	Haman	1884-1936	Hungarian Esperanto	Human Rights	Hungary	675
Katz	Sir Bernard	1911-2003	German Biophysist, Nobel Prize Winner	Scientists	Grenada	2489e
Katzenelson	Bert	1887-1944	Leader of Labor Zionist Org.	Zionists	Israel	713
Kaye	Danny	1913-1987	Singer, Actor	Actors, Entertainers	Gambia	774
Kaye	Danny	1913-1987	Singer, Actor	Actors, Entertainers	Grenada	2089
Kaye	Danny	1913-1987	Singer, Actor	Actors, Entertainers	Israel	1253
Kelsen	Hans	1881-1973	Austrian Legal Philosopher, Teacher	Philosophers	Austria	1190
Kelsen	Hans	1881-1973	Austrian Legal Philosopher, Teacher	Philosophers	Austria	1191
Kelson	Hans	1881-1973	Austrian Jurist, Philosopher	Philosophers	Austria	119
Kelson	Hans	1881-1973	Austrian Jurist, Philosopher	Philosophers	Austria	1191
Kelson	Hans	1881-1973	Jurist Costitution Law, Politics	Politicians	Austria	M1684
Kern	Jerome	1885-1945	"Showboat" Music Score by Jerome Kern	Actors, Entertainers	United States	2767
Kern	Joseph	1885-1945	American Composer of Musical Theatre, wrote music for "Showboat"	Composers , Musicians	United States	2110
Kern	Jerome	1885-1945	Musician, Writer	Musicians	United States	2767
Kestenbaum	Ofra	-Present	Israeli Graphic Artist, Subject on stamp by Asher Kalderon	Artists, Painters	Maldives	633
Khvoles	Rabbi Abram	1857-1931	Spiritual & Civic Leader- Lithuanian	Rabbis	Georgia	367
Kiesler	Frederick John (Jacob)	1890-1965	Austrian-American Artist, Sculptor, designer	Artists, Painters	Austria	2679
Killed Olympians	Munich Massacre	1972	Massacre at Munich Olympics of Jewish Athletes	Other	Guyana	3540a-i
Killed Olympians				Other	Guyana	3540a-i
Kinessit			Knessit	Special Issues	Venezuela	1598i
Kis	Danilo	1935-1989	Yugoslav Writer and Novelist	Writers	Montenegro	241
Kisch	Egon Erwin	1885-1948	Czech Writer, Journalist	Writers	East Germany	2470
Kisch	Egon Erwin	1885-1948	Czech Writer, Journalist	Writers	East Germany	2651
Kisch	Egon Erwin	1885-1948	Czech Writer, Journalist	Writers	Germany	1439
Kisling	Moshe	1891-1953	Landscape Artist	Artists, Painters	Bulgaria	3525
Kisling	Moshe	1891-1953	Painter - "Lady In Blue"	Artists, Painters	Israel	537
Kissenger	Henry	1923-date	American Statesman, Politician	Statesmen	Guyana	3016
Kissenger	Henry	1923-date	American Statesman, Politician	Statesmen	Guyana	3016
Kissenger	Henry	1923-date	American Statesman, Politician	Statesmen	Micronesia	379f
Klahr	Alfred	1904-1944	Austrian Comunist Politician, Journalist	Politicians	Germany	B94
Klausner	Joseph G.	1874-1958	Historian, Philosopher	Philosophers	Israel	804
Klemperer	Werner Otto	1920-2000	Comedian, Actor	Actors, Entertainers	Germany	9N502
Kogan	Moshe (Mossey)	1879-1943	Romanian Illustrator & Sculptor, Died in Auschwitz	Artists, Painters	Moldova	2004
Kollek	Teddy	1911-2007	Israli Politician, Jerusalem Mayor	National Government Leaders	Israel	1939
Komensky	Jan Amos	1592-1670	Czech Writer, Teacher, Scholar, Educator	Educator, Scholar	Czechoslavakia	509
Komensky	Jan Amos	1592-1670	Czech Writer, Teacher, Scholar, Educator	Educator, Scholar	Czechoslavakia	510
Kook	Rabbi Isaac	1865-1935	First Chief Rabbi of Israel	Rabbis	Israel	699
Koranyi	Sander	1866-1944	Hungarian Doctor	Scientists	Hungary	2276
Koranyi	Frigyes	1828-1913	Hungarian Physician, family name Kornfeldt	Scientists	Hungary	1103
Koranyi	Frigyes	1828-1913	Hungarian Physician, family name Kornfeldt	Scientists	Hungary	1498
Korczak	Janusz	1879-1942	Physician, Teacher, Writer	Rabbis	Israel	230
Korngold	Erich Wolfgang	1897-1957	Musician	Musicians	United States	3344
Kossak	Juliusz	1824-1899	Polish Artist	Artists, Painters	Israel	1772
Koufax	Sandy	1935-date	Baseball Star	Athletes	St. Vincent	2356
Koufax	Sandy	1935-date	Baseball Star	Athletes	St. Vincent	2356A-D
Krakauer	Leopold	1890-1954	Painter, Artist - "Thistles"	Artists, Painters	Israel	683
Kraus	Karl	1874-1936	Austrian Writer & Journalist	Writers	Austria	986
Kravitz	Duddy	1959-date	Movie of Jewish Life in Canada	Actors, Entertainers	Canada	1616b
Kreisky	Bruno	1911-1990	Austrian Politician, Foreign Minister	National Government Leaders	Austria	1527
Kronenberg	Leopold Stanislaw	1812-1678	Polish-Russian Banker, Jewish & Converted to Protestant	Financiers, Businessmen	Poland	4036
Kukovski	Yosef	1902-1969	Russian Artist, Painter - "The Last Way"	Artists, Painters	Israel	843

LAST NAME	FIRST NAME	DATES LIVED	FIELD OF KNOWLEDGE	HERO CLASSIFICATION	COUNTRY OF STAMP	SCOTT # OF STAMP
Kun (Kohn)	Bela	1886-1938	Hungarian Communist Revolutionary, Politician	Politicians	Hungary	2970
Kun (Kohn)	Bela	1886-1938	Hungarian Communist Revolutionary, Politician	Politicians	Russia	5431
La Guardia	Fiorello	1882-1947	New York Mayor for 3 Terms	National Government Leaders	Tanzania	1502
La Guardia	Fiorello	1882-1947	New York Mayor for 3 Terms	National Government Leaders	Tanzania	1502
La Guardia	Fiorello	1882-1947	Mayor of New York	National Government Leaders	United States	1397
Lahr	Bert	1895-1967	American actor, Played the Tin Man in Wizard of Oz	Actors, Entertainers	Mali	728
Lamaar	Hedy	1914-2000	Austrian American Hollywood Superstar	Actors, Entertainers	Austria	2296
Landau	Lev Davidovich	1908-1968	Soviet Physicist	Scientists	Israel	1330c
Landau	Lev Davidovich	1908-1968	Soviet Physicist	Scientists	Malagasy	1132g
Landau	Lev Davidovich	1908-1968	Soviet Physicist	Scientists	Malagasy	1132g
Landler	Jeno	1875-1928	Trade Union Official, Journalist	Journalists	Hungary	1402
Lang	Fritz	1890-1976	Austrian Filmmaker, Screenwriter	Writers	Dominica	944 M/S
Lasker	Emanuel	1868-1941	German Chess Master	Chess Masters	Cambodia	1390 M/S
Lasker	Emanuel	1868-1941	German Chess Master, Philosopher, Mathematician	Chess Masters	Laos	901E
Lassalle-Wolfson	Ferdinand Johann	1825-1964	German-Jewish Philosopher, Socialist, Jurist, Political Activist	Philosophers	Germany	1348
Laub	Ferdinand	1832-1875	Czech Violin Virtuosa	Composers , Musicians	Czechoslovakia	802
Laurel	Stan	1890-1965	English Actor, Writer, Director	Actors , Entertainers	Guyana	2544
Lavie	Arik	1927-2004	Musician	Musicians	Israel	1773J
Lehar	Franz	1870-1948	Austrian Composer of Operettas	Composers , Musicians	Austria	875
Lehar	Franz	1870-1948	Austrian Composer of Operettas	Composers , Musicians	Austria	1084
Lehar	Franz	1870-1948	Austrian-Hungarian Composer, Operettas	Composers , Musicians	Hungary	2022
Lerner	Alan Jay	1918-1986	Songwriter	Writers	United States	2770
Lerner	Alan Jay	1918-1986	Songwriter	Writers	United States	3346
Leuschner	Wilhelm	1890-1944	Politician- Executed in 1944	Politicians	Germany	1606
Levanon	Mordechai	1901-1968	Painter, Artist- "An Alley In Zefat"	Artists, Painters	Israel	684
Levertoff	Pricilla Denise	1923-1997	Poet, Book writer	Writers	United States	4661
Levi	Primo	1919-1987	Chemist, Writer, Holocaust Survivor	Writers	Italy	3158
Levi-Mortalani	Rita	1909-date	Italian Physiology Medicine Nobel Prize	Scientists	Sierre Leone	1844g
Levin	Rabbi Arys	1885-1969	Rabbi	Rabbis	Israel	803
Levi-Strauss	Claude	1908-2009	French Anthropologist, Ethnologist	Scientists	Brazil	3100
Levitan	Isaak	1860-1900	Painter	Artists, Painters	Russia	7235
Levitan	Isaac	1860-1900	Russian Landscape Painter	Artists, Painters	Russia	7235
Levy	Renee	1906-1943	French Resistance Fighter WW2, school teacher	Martyrs	France	1905
Lewandowski	Louis	1821-1894	German Composer of Synagogue Music	Composers , Musicians	German Demokratic Republic	2845
Lewis	Jerry	1926-date	American Comedian, Actor, Writer	Actors, Entertainers	Ghana	1909
Lieben	Robert Von	1878-1913	Austrian Physicist, Invented Telephone Amplifier	Inventors	Austria	BG150
Lieberrmann	Max	1847-1935	German Jewish Painter	Artists, Painters	Germany	431
Lieberrmann	Max	1847-1935	German Jewish Painter	Artists, Painters	Germany	1878
Lieberrmann	Max	1847-1935	German Jewish Painter	Artists, Painters	Germany	2970
Lilien	E. Moshe	1874-1925	Founder- Bezalel Academy of Art, Zionist themed art	Artists, Painters	Israel	625-627
Lippman	Walter	1889-1974	American Political Commontator	Broadcasting	United States	1849
Lippman	Gabriel	1845-1921	French Physicist & Inventor, Nobel in Physics	Scientists	Sweden	804
Lippman	Gabriel	1845-1921	French Physicist & Inventor, Nobel in Physics	Scientists	Sweden	806
Lippman	Gabriel	1845-1921	French Physicist & Inventor, Nobel in Physics	Scientists	Sweden	804A
Lippman	Gabriel	1845-1921	French Physicist & Inventor, Nobel in Physics	Scientists	Sweden	806A
Lishanski	Yoseph	1890-1917	Espionage Martyr	Martyrs	Israel	831D
Lissitsky	Lazar Markovich (EL)	1890-1941	Russian artist,designer, architect	Artists, Painters	Germany	2226
Loesser	Frank	1910-1969	Songwriter	Writers	United States	3350
Loew (Low) ben Bezael	Rabbi Judah	1526?-1609	Maharal of Prague, Talmudic Scholar , Philosopher	Philosophers	Czechoslovakia	3423
Loewi	Otto	1873-1961	German Pharmacologist	Scientists	Austria	942
Lowy	Frank	1930-present	Australlian-Israeli Businessman	Financiers, Businessmen	Australia	2778
Lubin	Aryeh	1897-1980	Painter, Artist -Tel Aviv Landscape	Artists, Painters	Israel	815
Lumier	Auguste	1862-1954	Film Maker, Invented Moving Pictures	Inventors	France	771
Lumier	Louis	1864-1948	Film Maker, Invented Moving Pictures	Inventors	France	771
Luxemberg	Rosa	1871-1919	Economist, Philosopher	Philosophers	German Demokratic Republic	419
Luxemberg	Rosa	1870-1919	Socialist Leader	Socialogists	Israel	1362c
Luxemburg	Rosa	1871-1919	Economist, Philosopher, Socialist leader	Philosophers	Germany	MI478
Maazel	Lorin	1930-2014	American Conductor, Composer	Composers , Musicians	Austria	1976
Maccabaeus	Judas	190BC-160BC	Jewish Warrior	Military	Israel	209
Madgearu	Virgil	1887-1940	Victim of Nazi Terrorism, left-wing politician	National Government Leaders	Romania	B262
Mahler	Gustav	1860-1911	Composer	Composers , Musicians	Austria	654
Mahler	Gustav	1860-1911	Composer	Composers , Musicians	Austria	3118
Mahler	Gustav	1860-1911	Composer	Composers , Musicians	Austria	3119
Mahler	Gustav	1860-1911	Composer	Composers , Musicians	Czechoslavakia	3119
Mahler	Gustav	1860-1911	Composer	Composers , Musicians	Hungary	2942
Mahler	Gustav	1860-1911	Composer	Composers , Musicians	Israel	1274

LAST NAME	FIRST NAME	DATES LIVED	FIELD OF KNOWLEDGE	HERO CLASSIFICATION	COUNTRY OF STAMP	SCOTT # OF STAMP
Mahler	Gustav	1860-1911	Composer	Composers , Musicians	Monaco	2571
Mahr	Ernst	1887-1930	Leading Biologist, Taxonomist, Historian	Scientists	East Germany	1852 FDC
Maimon	Rabbi Judah Leib	1875-1962	Rabbi	Rabbis	Israel	1011
Maimon (Maimonides)	Rabbi Moshe ban	1135-1204	Rabbi & Philosopher	Philosophers	Israel	74
Maimonadis	Rabbi Moshe ben	1135-1204	Rabbi & Philosopher	Philosophers	Grenada	719
Maimonadis	Rabbi Moshe ben	1135-1204	Rabbi & Philosopher	Philosophers	Grenada	402A S/S
Maimonides	Moses	1135-1204	Philosopher, stamp is 800th Anniv. of death	Philosophers	Grenada Grenadines	2611
Mandel	Georges	1885-1944	French Political Journalist	Writers	France	1104 Imperf
Mandel	Georges	1885-1944	French Political Journalist	Writers	France	1104 Perf.
Manin	Daniel	1810-1883	Italian Patriot Political Leader	Politicians	Italy	499
Manor	Ehud	1941-2005	Musician	Musicians	Israel	1773I
Mapu	Abraham	1808-1867	Novelist, Historian	Writers	Israel	376
Marcus	Siegfried Samuel	1831-1898	German Inventor- Marcus Car	Inventors	Austria	906
Maric	Mileva	1875-1948	married Einstein, Serbian Physicist, Never Converted	Scientists	Serbia	660
Marshak	Samuel	1887-1964	Russian Author, Poet, Translator	Writers	Russia	5612
Marshall	Samuel	1900-1977	American Military Historian	Military	Russia	5612
Martyrs for Independence			Heroes for Jewish Freedom	Martyrs	Israel [20]	831 Sheet
Marx	Groucho	1890-1977	Comedian Actor	Actors, Enterainers	Gambia	776
Marx	Gummo	1893-1977	Comedian, Actor, Movies	Actors, Entertainers	Gambia	776
Marx	Harpo	1888-1964	Comedian, Actor, Movies	Actors, Entertainers	Gambia	776
Marx	Chico	1887-1961	Comedian, Actor, Movies	Actors, Entertainers	Gambia	776
Marx	Groucho	1890-1977	Comedian Actor	Actors, Entertainers	Ghana	1942
Marx	Groucho	1890-1977	Comedian Actor	Actors, Entertainers	Grenada	2553
Marx	Groucho	1890-1977	Comedian Actor	Actors, Entertainers	Guyana	2545
Marx	Chico	1887-1961	Comedian, Actor, Movies	Actors, Entertainers	Israel	776
Marx	Gummo	1893-1977	Comedian, Actor, Movies	Actors, Entertainers	Israel	776
Marx	Harpo	1888-1964	Comedian, Actor, Movies	Actors, Entertainers	Israel	776
Marx	Chico	1887-1961	Comedian, Actor, Movies	Actors, Entertainers	Israel	1253
Marx	Gummo	1893-1977	Comedian, Actor, Movies	Actors, Entertainers	Israel	1253
Marx	Harpo	1888-1964	Comedian, Actor, Movies	Actors, Entertainers	Israel	1253
Marx	Groucho	1890-1977	Comedian, Actor, Tv show Host	Actors, Entertainers	United States	4414H
Marx	Karl H.	1818-1883	Inventor of Marxism, Phtosopher, Sociologist	Socialogst	Cuba	2564
Marx	Karl H.	1818-1883	Inventor of Marxism, Philosopher, Sociologist, 60kon	Sociologists	Russia	2057
Marx	Karl H.	1818-1883	Inventor of Marxism, Philosopher, Sociologist- 1pye	Sociologists	Russia	2058
Marzouk	Moshe	1927-1955	Martyr For Independence	Martyrs	Israel	831R
Masaryk	Thomas	1850-1937	Lawyer, Defender of Zionists and Jewish Rights	Human Rights	Czechoslovakia	91
Masaryk	Tomas Garrigue	1850-1937	Lawyer, defender of Zionists and Jewish rights	Human Rights	Czechoslovakia	2772
Masaryk	Tomas Garrigue	1850-1937	Lawyer, defender of Zionists and Jewish rights	Human Rights	United States	1147
Masaryk	Tomas Garrigue	1850-1937	Lawyer, defender of Zionists and Jewish rights	Human Rights	United States	1148
Masaryk	Tomas Garrigue	1850-1937	Lawyer, Defender of Human Rights, Pres. Of Czechoslavakia	Human Rights	United States	1147-48
Masaryk	Tomas	1850-1937	Lawyer, defender of Zionists and Jewish rights 1920-gm-blu	National Government Leaders	Czechoslovakia	61
Masaryk	Tomas	1850-1937	Lawyer, defender of Zionists and Jewish rights 1923 grn, 1st Pres. Of Czech.	National Government Leaders	Czechoslovakia	91
Masaryk	Tomas Garrigue	1850-1937	Lawyer, defender of Zionists and Jewish rights, 1st Pres. Of Czech.	National Government Leaders	Czechoslovakia	247
Matthau	Walter	1920-2000	American Actor	Actors, Entertainers	Gambia	1351b
Matthau	Walter	1920-2000	American Actor	Actors, Entertainers	Gambia	1351b
Mauycy	Gottlieb	1856-1879	Polish Artist, Painter	Artists, Painters	Israel	569
Mayer	Helene	1910-1953	Germany Olympic Fencer, World Champion	Athletes	Germany	B436
Mehta	Zubin	1936-date	India Born Musician, Conductor	Musicians	Maldive Islands	1821 M/S
Meir	Golda	1898-1978	Prime Minister of Israel	National Government Leaders	Israel	770
Meir	Golda	1898-1978	Prime Minister of Israel	National Government Leaders	St. Thomas & Prince Islands	2140 Sheet
Meir	Jacob	1856-1939	Rabbi	Rabbis	Israel	1648
Meir	Jacob	1856-1939	Rabbi	Rabbis	Israel	1648
Meitner	Lise	1878-1968	Austrian Physicist -Radioactive Physics	Scientists	Austria	1093
Meitner	Lise	1878-1968	Austrian Swedish Physicist	Scientists	Germany	9N524
Melnikov	Abraham	1892-1960	Artist	Artists, Painters	Israel	864
Menahem	Shemi	1879-1951	Artist	Artists, Painters	Israel	481
Mendelssohn	Felix	1809-1847	Compcser	Composers , Musicians	Bulgaria	3988c
Mendelssohn	Felix	1809-1847	Compcser	Composers , Musicians	Deutch Bundenpost	4804E
Mendelssohn	Felix	1809-1847	Compcser	Composers , Musicians	Deutchland Germany	1980
Mendelssohn	Felix	1809-1847	Compcser	Composers , Musicians	Israel	1274
Mendelssohn	Felix	1809-1847	Compcser	Composers , Musicians	Monaco	2527
Mendelssohn	Moses	1729-1786	Philosopher	Philosophers	Germany	9N429
Mendelsson	Felix	1809-1847	Compcser	Composers , Musicians	German Democratic Republic	421
Mendelsson	Felix	1809-1847	Compcser	Comooers , Musicians	German Democratic Republic	2393
Mendelsson	Felix	1809-1847	Compcser	Comoosers , Musicians	German Democratic Republic	1984 M/S

LAST NAME	FIRST NAME	DATES LIVED	FIELD OF KNOWLEDGE	HERO CLASSIFICATION	COUNTRY OF STAMP	SCOTT # OF STAMP
Menorah	Maria la Bianca Synagogue			Other	Spain	2972-3
Menorah		1937-1945	Symbol	Other	St. Thomas & Prince Islands	2245 Sheet
Menorah			Menorah	Special Issues	Venezuela	598a
Menuhin	Yehudi	1916-1999	American born Violinist, Conductor, Stamp Collector	Composers , Musicians	Kyrgyzstak	Sc 38, KEP M46
Meridor	Ya'acov	1913-1995	Government	Statesmen	Israel	1518
Messas	Chalom	1909-2003	Rabbi	Rabbis	Israel	1695
Metchenikof	Elle	1845-1916	Russian Scientist, Biologist	Scientists	France	B398
Metchenlkof	Elle	1845-1916	Russian Scientist, Biologist	Scientists	Russia	6000
Meyer	Ernst	1791-1858	German Botanist, Biologist	Scientists	East Germany	1852
Meyer (Mayr)	Ernst	1904-2005	Biologist, Philosopher of Biology, Science Historian	Scientists	East Germany	1852
Meyerhof	Otto	1884-1951	German Born Physicist, Nobel Winner	Scientists	Grenada	2490f
Micheson	Albert	1852-1931	American Physicist, Studied Speed of Light	Scientists	Sweden	769
Midler	Bette	1945-date	American Singer, Actress, Comedian	Musicians	Mall	730 M/S
Milhaud	Darius	1892-1974	Composer,	Composers , Musicians	France	1975
Milhaud	Darius	1892-1974	Composer	Composers , Musicians	Israel	1232
Milk	Harvey	1930-1978	American Municipal Politician, openly gay	Politicians	United States	4906
Millo	Joseph	1916-1997	Theatre	Actors, Entertainers	Israel	1624
Modigellani	Amedeo	1884-1920	Italian Economist, Artist	Artists, Painters	France	1693
Mohilewer	Samuel	1824-1898	Rabbi	Rabbis	Israel	1742
Monash	General John	1865-1931	Civil Engineer, Australian Commander	National Government Leaders	Australia	390
Monroe	Marilyn	1926-1962	Actress	Actors, Entertainers	Antigua	1041
Monroe	Marilyn	1926-1962	Actress	Actors, Entertainers	Mali	696
Monroe	Marilyn	1926-1962	Actress	Actors, Entertainers	Marshall Islands (12)	592 Sheet
Monroe	Marilyn	1926-1962	Actress	Actors, Entertainers	United States	2967
Montaigne	Michel de	1533-1592	Philosopher	Philosophers	France	B161
Montefiore	Moses	1784-1885	First Knighted Jew	Other	Israel	777
Monus	Illes	1888-1944	Journalist- Party Leader	Writers	Hungary	3118
Monus	Illes	1888-1944	Journalist- Party Leader	Writers	Hungary	B180
Morgemthau	Henry	1856-1946	American Lawyer, Businessman, US Ambassador to Ottoman Empire	National Government Leaders	Armenia	1036
Moses	Nicholus Poussin	1594-1665	French Painter	Artists, Painters	France	2435
Moses		1391BC-1271BC	Prophet, Law Giver	Prophets	Grenada	678
Moses		1391-1271 BC	Prophet, Law Giver	Special Issues	Palau	396h
Moses		1391-1271BC	Prophet, Law Giver	Special Issues	Palau	396i
Moses			Moses	Special Issues	Venezuela	598b
Mostel	Zero	1915-1977	American Film & Stage Actor	Actors, Entertainers	Antigua & Barbuda	2037c
Mottelson	Benjamin	1827-1877	Geneology	Scientists	Maldive Islands	2116b
Mottelson	Benjamin	1827-1877	Geneolcgy	Scientists	Maldive Islands	2116b
Mourad	Leila	1918-1965	Father of Jewish descent, Egyptian Singer-Actress	Actors, Singers	Egypt	1731
Mozart	Wolfgang	1756-1791	Austrian Composer	Composers , Musicians	Austria	609
Mozart	Wolfgang	1756-1791	Austrian Composer	Composers , Musicians	Israel	1101
Nagler	Marianne M.	1943-present	Artist, designed Jewish themed stamp for Denmark, "Sabbath Candles"	Artists, Painters	Denmark	766
Najdorf	Manuel (Miguel)	1910-1997	born Mendel, International Chess Master	Chess Masters	Argentina	2633
Nakar	Meir	1926-1947	Martyr For Independence	Martyrs	Israel	831K
Nathans	Daniel	1928-1999	American Microbiologist	Scientists	Israel	2113f
Nebuchadnezzar		634-562BC	Prophet, Law Giver	Special Issues	Palau	396ac
Nemes	Endre	1909-1985	Surrealist Artist, Enamels used in art	Artists, Painters	Slovakia	255 M/S
Netter	Charles	1826-1882	College Founder, Zionist Leader	Zionists	Israel	417
Neuman	John Von	1903-1957	Hungarian-American Mathematician, Physicist, Inventor	Scientists	United States	3908
Newman	Paul	1925-2008	Famous Actor, Friend of Jews, Father Jewish, Philanthropist, Director	Actors, Entertainers	St. Thomas & Prince Islands	1956
Newman	Alfred	1907-1970	Musician	Musicians	United States	3343
Newton-John	Olivia	1948-present	English-Australian singer, writer, grandfather Jewish	Actors, Entertainers	Australia	B6
Nimon(Startrek)	Leonard Nimoy	1931-date	American Actor	Actors, Entertainers	St. Vincent	2544-5
Noah			Famous for Ark Building Story With Stamps - 25	Special Issues	Palau	396c
Noah's Ark		2900BC	Noah's Ark	Special Issues	St. Vincent (25)	1152a-y
Nordau	Max	1849-1923	Hungarian Zionist Leader, Physician, Author	Zionists	Israel	780
Nussbaum	Felix	1904-1944	German Jewish Artist, died Auschwitz	Artists, Painters	Germany	2303
Offenbach	Jaques	1819-1880	French Composer, Cellist	Composers , Musicians	Belgium Congo	C288
Offenbach	Jaques	1819-1880	French Composer, Cellist	Composers , Musicians	Belgium Congo	C288
Offenbach	Jaques	1819-1880	French Composer, Cellist	Composers , Musicians	Benin	499
Offenbach	Jaques	1819-1880	French Composer, Cellist	Composers , Musicians	Benin	500
Offenbach	Jaques	1819-1880	French Composer, Cellist	Composers , Musicians	France	B536
Olbracht	Ivan	1882-1952	born Kamil Zeman, Novelist, Czech writer	Writers	Czechoslovakia	781
Olivetti	Camilo	1868-1943	Inventor of the typewriter, Electrical Engineer	Inventors	Italy	2851 FDC
Ophir	Shai	1928-1987	Israel Theatre Actor	Actors, Entertainers	Israel	1626

242

LAST NAME	FIRST NAME	DATES LIVED	FIELD OF KNOWLEDGE	HERO CLASSIFICATION	COUNTRY OF STAMP	SCOTT # OF STAMP
Oppenheim	Moritz D.	1800-1882	Abstractionist, Painter - "Hannukah"	Artists, Painters	Israel	567
Oppenheimer	Franz	1864-1943	German Sociologist, Political Economist, Writer of the States	Sociologists	Germany	837
Orloff	Chana	1888-1968	Sculptor, Painter - "Mother & Child"	Artists, Painters	Israel	538
Orloff	Chana	1888-1968	Artist	Artists, Painters	Israel	865
Ormandy	Eugene	1899-1985	Hungarian Musician, Conductor	Musicians	United States	3161
Ouziel	Rabbi	1880-1953	Rabbi Hero	Rabbis	Israel	700
Paldi	Israel	1892-1979	Israeli Artist, Painter	Artists, Painters	Israel	817
Pann	Abe	1883-1963	Artist - "Young Girl"	Artists, Painters	Israel	480
Padineau	Louis J.	1786-1871	Legislative member, Patriot	National Government Leaders	Canada	539
Pappenheim	Bertha	1859-1936	Austrian feminist, founder Jewish Womens Assoc.	Psychoanalists	Germany	B341
Pasternak	Boris	1890-1960	Russian Artist, Painter	Artists, Painters	Russia	5939
Pauli	Wolfgang	1900-1958	Austrian Physicist, Quantum Physics	Scientists	Grenada	2489d
Peace Corps			Special First Day Cover, Wrting In Hebrew -Shalom (Peace)	Other	United States	1447
Pen	Y.M.		Famous Painter, 'Old Jew Reading Yiddish'	Artists, Painters	Belarus	530
Peretz	Issac Lieb	1852-1915	Yiddish Writer	Writers	Israel	1269i
Picasso	Pablo	1881-1973	Painter of Oils, Pastels, Drawings	Artists, Painters	Marshall Islands	627m
Pierard	Louis J.	1886-1951	Belgian Writer, Artist, Sculptor	Writers	Belgium	860
Pleskow	Eric	1924-oresent	Film Producer, Media Executive	Film	Austria	2495
Pinsker	Leon	1821-1891	Hovevei Zion Founder	Zionists	Israel	880
Pintille	Ilie	1903-1940	Victim of Nazi Terrorism, Labor Party Movement	National Government Leaders	Romania	B264
Pintilie Bernath	Andrei Ilie	1903-1940	Victim of Nazis Military War, Romanian	Martyrs	Romania	B267
Pisaro	Camillo	1830-1903	Danish-French Impressionist painter	Artists, Painters	France	1729
Polanyi	PaulC.	1929-oresent	Chemist, Nobel Prize Winner	Scientists	Canada	468 Bklt.
Polanyi	Paul C.	1929-present	Chemist, Nobel Prize Winner	Scientists	Canada	489 FDC
Politzer	Adam	1835-1920	20th Century Otology Studies	Scientists	Austria	1326
Politzer	Dr. Adam	1835-1920	Hungarian-Austrian Physician	Scientists	Austria	1326
Polus	David	1886-1947	Ukranian Artist, Sculetor	Artists, Painters	Israel	863
Popper	Julius	1857-1893	Romanian Engineer, Exolorer	Other	Romania	3393
Porgy & Bess			Opera By Ira & George Gershwin	Musicians	United States	2768
Portal	Antoine	1742-1832	French Doctor, Historian, Anatomist, Founded Royal Acad. Of Medicine	Scientists	France	1699
Praying At the Wall			Praying at the Wailing Wall	Symbol	Venezuela	1588g
Preminger	Otto	1905-1986	Austrian-Hungarian Theatre & Film Director	Film	Austria	2239
Prestes	Olga Gutman Benario	1908-1944	German-Brazilian Communist Militant, Executed	Martyrs	Germany	B52
Proust	Marcel	1871-1922	French Novelist, Critic	Writers	France	B396
Pulitzer	Joseph	1847-1947	Hungarian Newspaper Publisher, Journalist, Prize Named After Him	Writers	United States	946
Rabin	Yitzhak	1922-1995	Prime Minister	National Government Leaders	Israel	1249
Rabin	Yitzhak	1922-1995	Prime Minister	National Government Leaders	Israel	1608
Rabin	Yitzhak	1922-1995	Nobel Peace Prize - 1994	National Government Leaders	St. Thomas & Prince Islands	2143 Sheet
Racah	Giulio	1909-1965	Physicist	Scientists	Israel	1165
Racosi	Matyas	1892-1971	Hungarian Politician	Politicians	Hungary	987
Racosi	Matyas	1892-1971	Hungarian Politician	Politicians	Hungary	998
Radcliffe	Daniel	1989-oresent	English Actor, Harry Potter	Actors, Entertainers	France	3303
Ramon	Ilan	1954-2003	Astronaut	Astronaut	Israel	1552
Rand	Ayn	1905-82	Writer	Writers	United States	3308
Rashi	Moses	1040-1105	Scholar and Bible Interpreter, Schlomo Yitzchaki	Writers	France	3088
Rashi	Moses	1040-1105	Scholar and Bible Interpreter, Schlomo Yitzchaki	Writers	France	1012
Rathenau	Walter	1867-1922	German-Jewish Statesman	National Government Leaders	Germany	9N86
Raziel	David	1910-1941	British Underground Hero	Underground Heroes	Israel	690
Recanati	Leon Yehuda	1890-1945	Financier	Financiers, Businessmen	Israel	918
Red Sea Parting			Parting off the! Red Sea Story on Stamps - 24	Special Issues	Guyana (24)	1994 Sheet
Reik	Havivah	1914-1944	Executed Agent	Underground Heroes	Israel	994
Reinhardt	Max	1873-1943	Theatrical Director	Actors, Entertainers	Austria	952
Reinhardt	Max	1873-1943	Theatrical Director	Actors, Entertainers	Germany	1428
Rememberance of Holocaust Victims		1937-1945	Symbol	Other	St. Thomas & Prince Islands	2245 Sheet
Rene	Roy	1891-1954	Australian comedian- born Harry van der Sluys	Comedians	Australia	1142
Ringelblum	Emanuel	1900-1944	Historian Writer	Writers	Israel	1553
Robertson	Robbie	1943-present	Canadian musician, Jewish Father, Singer, Songwriter	Actors, Entertainers	Canada	2482B
Robinson	Edward G.	1893-1973	American Stage & Film Actor	Actors, Entertainers	Grenada Grenadines	2124c-d
Robinson (Goldenberg)	Edward G. (Emanuel)	1893-1973	Romanian born Actor, Performed in over 100 movies	Actors, Entertainers	United States	3446
Rodgers	Richard	1902-1979	Songwriter	Writers	United States	3348
Rokach	Israel	1896-1959	Government	Politicians	Israel	1713
Rosen	Pinchas	1887-1978	Minister of Justice	National Government Leaders	Israel	974
Rosenberg	Ethel	1915-1953	Actress, Singer, Executed for Conspiracy	Actors, Entertainers	Cuba	C313
Rosenblum	Yair	1944-1996	Musician	Musicans	Israel	1773G
Rosenfield	Fanny	1904-1969	Canadian Athlete, Runner	Athletes	Canada	1610

LAST NAME	FIRST NAME	DATES LIVED	FIELD OF KNOWLEDGE	HERO CLASSIFICATION	COUNTRY OF STAMP	SCOTT # OF STAMP
Rosenthal	C. D.	1820-1851	Romanian Painter, Sculptor	Artists, Painters	Romania	Mi 1270-71
Rosenthal	C. D.	1820-1851	Romanian Painter, Sculptor	Artists, Painters	Romania	Mi1268-69
Rothschild	Baron Edmond De	1845-1934	French Zionist, Banker	Zionists	Israel	90
Rovina	Hannah	1889-1980	Actress	Actors, Entertainers	Israel	1102
Rowe	Leo	1871-1946	Doctor, Latin Educator Donor, Pan-Amer. Dir.	Educator, Scholar	Nicaragua	C253
Rozca	Florance	1906-1942	Journalist, Freedom Fighter	Martyrs	Hungary	B181
Rubens	Peter Paul	1577-1640	Flemish Artist, Painter	Artists, Painters	Grenada Grenadines	1231
Rubens	Peter Paul	1577-1640	Flemish Artist Painter	Artists, Painters	Grenada Grenadines	1226-7
Rubens	Peter Paul	1577-1640	Flemish Artist, Painter	Artists, Painters	Grenada Grenadines	1226-7
Rubenstein	Arthur	1887-1982	Pianist	Musicians	Israel	935
Rubin	Reuven	1893-1974	Painter, Artist - "Dancers Of Meron"	Artists, Painters	Israel	599
Rubinstein	Anton G.	1829-1894	Russian Pianist, Conductor, Composer	Composers , Musicians	Russia	1745
Rumkowski	Chaim	1877-1944	Polish Businessman, murdered-Auschwitz, Lotz Ghetto Stamps	Financier, Businessman	Russia	1993 PC
Ruppin	Arthur	1876-1943	Zionist Hero & Leader	Zionists	Israel	740
Ruth			Biblical Woman	Other	Israel	886
Ruth & Naomi			Prophet, Law Giver	Special Issues	Palau	3960
Ryder	Winona	1971-present	American Singer, Actress	Actors, Entertainers	Abkhasia	1999 Illegal Sheet
Sabin	Albert	1906-1933	American Medical Researcher, Polio Vaccine	Scientists	Brazil	2467
Sachs	Nellie	1891-1970	German Literature, Playwrite	Writers	Germany	1895
Sacks	Nellie	1891-1970	German Literature, Playwrite	Writers	Sweden	2399b
Sadeh	Yitzhak	1890-1952	Underground Hero, Military	Underground Heroes	Israel	691
Sagvari	Endre	1913-1944	Hungarian Resistance Fighter	Martyrs	Hungary	B186
Salant	Samuel	1816-1909	Rabbi	Rabbis	Israel	1847
Salih	Shalom	1934-1952	Martyr For Independence	Martyrs	Israel	831S
Salk	Dr. Jonas	1914-1995	Co- inventor of Polio Vaccine, researcher	Scientists	Dominica	2004
Salk	Jonus	1914-1995	American Medical Researcher, Polio Vaccine	Scientists	Niger	1998
Salk	Jonus	1914-1995	American Medical Researcher, Polio Vaccine	Scientists	Niger	1998
Salk	Jonus	1914-1995	American Medical Researcher, Polio Vaccine	Scientists	Tanzania	1479
Salk	Jonus	1914-1995	American Medical Researcher, Polio Vaccine	Scientists	Transkei	261
Samson			Last Judge of Israel	National Government Leaders	Israel	208
Samson			Prophet, Law Giver	Special Issues	Palau	396n
Samuelson	Paul	1915-2009	American Economist -Nobel Prize winner	Scientists	Guine-Bissau	2837 M/S
Sarbu	Filimon	1916-1941	Victim of Nazi Terrorism, Anti-Facist	Human Rights	Romania	B266
Sassoon	Sigfried	1886-1967	English Poet, Writer,m. Soldier	Writers	St. Helena	971
Saul			King of Israel	National Government Leaders	Israel	184
Saul			Prophet, Law Giver	Special Issues	Palau	396b
Saul			Prophet, Law Giver	Special Issues	Palau	396q
Schachter	Leo	1914-1995	NY- Israeli Diamond merchant, named Leo Diamond	Financiers, Businessmen	Gambia	2774
Schaft	Johanna Jannetje	1920-1945	Dutch Communist Resistance Fighter. Not Jewish but fought for a lot 20+10	Martyrs	Germany	B86
Schatz	Boris	1867-1932	Lithuanian Sculptor, Artist - "The Scribe"	Artists, Painters	Israel	479
Schindler	Oskar	1908-1974	Industrialist, Saved Jews from the Holacaust	Financiers, Businessmen	Germany	FDC2481
Schindler	Oskar	1908-1974	Industrialist, Saved Jews from the Holacaust	Financiers, Businessmen	Germany	FDC2481
Schlonsky	Avraham	1900-1973	Hebrew Writer, Poet	Writers	Israel	1319 M/S
Schmeling	Max	1905-2005	German boxing World Heavyweight Champion	Athletes	Austria	1986
Schmeling	Max	1905-2005	German boxing World Heavyweight Champion	Athletes	Germany	2354
Schmidt	Joseph	1904-1942	Austrian- Hungarian Opera Singer and Cantor, Tenor	Actors, Entertainers	Germany	2274
Schnitzer	Arthur	1862-1931	Austrian Author and Dramatist	Writers	Austria	1396
Schoenberg	Arnold	1874-1951	Austrian Hungarian composer, painter	Composers , Musicians	Austria	1001
Schoenberg	Arnold	1874-1951	Austrian Hungarian composer, painter	Composers , Musicians	Israel	1231
Schonerz	Zoltan	1905-1942	Engineer	Scientists	Hungary	B181
Schuler	Else Lasker	1869-1945	Writer, Short Stories, Novelist, Playwright	Writers	Germany	1155
Schwartz	David	1845-1897	Inventor of Dirigbl Airship	Inventors	Hungary	C57
Schwimmer	Louis	1900-1975	Designed the 4 Chaplains US Stamp, 1st. US stamp with Jewish Person	Artists, Painters	United States	956
Sefarim	Mendele Mokher	1835-1917	Grandfather of Yiddish Literature	Writers	Israel	1269n
Segal	Laser	1891-1957	Brazilian Painter, Artist and Birth Centinary	Artists, Painters	Brazil	2339
Sellers	Peter	1925-1980	British Theatre, Movies	Actors, Entertainers	Dominica	1845
Sellers	Peter	1925-1980	British Theatre, Movies	Actors, Entertainers	Israel	1253
Sellers	Peter	1925-1980	British Theatre, Movies	Film	Israel	1253
Senesh	Chana	1921-1944	Parachutist, JNF Stamp, WW2, poet	Martyrs	Israel	GE206
Sereni	Enzohayyim	1905-1944	Executed Agent	Other	Israel	995
Serf	Barbara (Monique)	1930-1997	Singer	Musicians	France	2824
Shabtai	Yaacov	1934-1981	Wrote Sketches, Plays, & Novels	Writers	Israel	1269h
Sharett	Moshe	1894-1965	Prime Minister of Israel	National Government Leaders	Israel	360
Shaw	Artie	1910-2004	American Jazz Composer, Band Leader	Composers , Musicians	Dominica	1860
Shazar	Zalman	1889-1974	President of Israel	National Government Leaders	Israel	571

244

LAST NAME	FIRST NAME	DATES LIVED	FIELD OF KNOWLEDGE	HERO CLASSIFICATION	COUNTRY OF STAMP	SCOTT # OF STAMP
Shazar	Zalman	1889-1974	Author, Poet, President of Israel, Politician	National Government Leaders	Uruguay	C287
Shelton (Schechtel)	Sidney (Sheldon)	1917-2007	American writer, playwright, producer	Writers	Guyana	3453
Shemer	Naomi	1930-2004	Musician	Musicians	Israel	1773E
Shionsky	Abraham	1900-1973	Hebrew Writer, Poet	Writers	Israel	1269g
Shochat	Mania	1880-1961	Russian Politician	Politicians	Israel	409
Shofar Blowing			Shofar Blowing	Special Issues	Venezuela	1598e
Shore	Dinah	1916-1994	Singer, Actress	Actors, Entertainers	Antigua & Barbuda	2014
Shore	Dinah	1916-1994	Singer, Actress	Actors, Entertainers	Grenada Grenadines	1419
Shore	Dinah	1916-1994	Singer, Actress	Actors Entertainers	United States	4414-I
Shwarz	David	1850-1897	Inventor of 1st Aluminum Dirigible, Croation-Hungarian	Inventors	Cuba	3325
Signoret	Simore	1921-1985	French Theatre, Movies	Actors, Entertainers	France	B685
Signoret	Simore	1921-1985	French Theatre, Movies	Actors, Entertainers	Israel	1253
Signoret	Simore	1921-1985	French Theatre, Movies	Film	Israel	1253
Sills	Beverly	1929-2007	American Operatic Soprano	Actors, Entertainers	St. Vincent	2509
Sills	Beverly	1929-2007	American Operatic Soprano	Actors, Entertainers	St. Vincent	2509
Silver	Abba Hillel	1893-1963	Statesman	Statesmen	Israel	778
Silvers	Phil	1911-1985	American Actor, Comedian	Actors, Entertainers	Grenada	2088
Silvers	Phil	1911-1985	American Actor, Comedian	Actors, Entertainers	United States	4414L
Simon	Carly	1945-present	Singer, songwriter, author, musician	Musicians	Mail	MI145
Simon	Bar Kokhba	132CE	Jewish Leader of Israel	National Government Leaders	Israel	210
Skutecky	Dominik	1849-1921	Painter	Artists, Painters	Slovakia	341
Smorgon	Victor	1913-2009	Australian Industrialist, father had kosher deli	Financiers, Businessmen	Australia	2778A
Smorgon	Loti	1919-2013	Philanthropist, Meat, steel industry	Financiers, Businessmen	Australia	2778A
Smoria	Moshe	1888-1961	President of Supreme Court	National Government Leaders	Israel	1023
Sneh	Dr. Moshe	1909-1972	Underground Hero, Military Figuro	Underground Heroes	Israel	689
Sofer	Chatam	1762-1839	Rabbi, Teacher	Rabbis	Slovakia	196
Soloman			King of Israel	National Government Leaders	Israel	186
Solomon	Haym	1740-1785	Financed Continental Army	Financiers, Businessmen	United States	1561
Solomon		967BC	Prophet, Law Giver	Special Issues	Palau	396u
Solomon		967BC	Prophet, Law Giver	Special Issues	Palau	396v
Soros (Swartz)	George (Gyorgy)	1930-present	Jewish Business Magnate, Philanthropist	Financiers, Businessmen	Micronesia (25)	389a-p, 389n
Soutine	Chaim	1893-1943	Painter, Artist, Expressionist - "Girl In Blue"	Artists, Painters	Israel	539
Spasky	Boris	1937-date	Chess Master	Chess Masters	St. Vincent	1562e
Spinoza	Baruch	1632-1677	Philosopher	Philosophers	Israel	1485
Spinoza	Baruch	1632-1677	Philosopher	Philosophers	Netherlands	567
Spitz	Mark	1950-present	American Swimmer, Won 7 Gold Medals	Athletes	Fujeira	1454
Spitz	Mark	1950-date	Seven Gold Medals in Swimming	Athletes	Grenada Grenadines	1695
Spitz	Mark	1950-present	American Swimmer, Won 7 Gold Medals	Athletes	Grenada Grenadines	1695
Spitz	Mark	1950-date	Seven Gold Medals in Swimming	Athletes	Grenada Grenadines	1885
Spitz	Mark	1950-date	Seven Gold Medals in Swimming	Athletes	Grenada Grenadines	1885
Sprinzak	Joseph	1885-1959	Speaker of Kinesset	Statesmen	France	946
St. Therese of Avila		1515-1582	Jewish grandmother,Author, Spanish Mystic	Writers	Romania F-167	1846
Stahi	Constantin Daniel	1844-1920	Romanian Painter, Artist	Artists, Painters	Romania F167	MI1267-71
Star of David	Santa Maria ia Bianca Synagogue			Other	Spain (2)	2972
Star of David	Maria la Bianca Synagogue			Other	Spain (2)	2973
Star of David			Symbol	Other	St. Thomas & Prince Islands	2245 Sheet
State of Israel		1937-1945	50th Anniversary State of Israel	Special Issues	Venezuela	1598 Sheet
Stein	Gertrude	1881-1973	Artist	Artists, Painters	Uganda	1186
Stein	Gertrude	1881-1973	Artist	Artists, Painters	Uganda	1186
Stein	Edith	1891-1942	German Philosopher, Converted to Roman Catholic	Philosophers	Germany	1385
Steinberger	Jack	1921-date	German-American Physicist	Scientists	Antigua	1945d
Steiner	Max	1888-1971	Musician	Musicians	United States	3339
Steinetz	Wilhelm	1836-1900	Austrian-American Chess Master	Chess Masters	Cambodia	1389
Steinhardt	Jacob	1887-1968	Woodcut Artist, Painter - "Old Jerusalem"	Artists, Painters	Israel	482
Steinitz	Wilhelm	1836-1900	Austrian-American Chess Master	Chess Masters	Laos	901D
Steinitz	Wilhelm	1836-1900	Austrian American Chess Master	Chess Masters	St. Vincent	1562c
Steinitz	Wilhelm	1836-1900	Austrian American Chess Master	Chess Masters	St. Vincent	1562c
Stern	Otto	1888-1969	German Physicist & Nobel Prize Winner	Scientists	Antigua	1945f
Stern	Otto	1888-1969	German Physicist & Nobel Prize Winner.	Scientists	Antigua	1945f
Stern	Abraham	1907-1942	Underground Heroes	Underground Heroes	Israel	692
Stolz	Robert	1880-1980	Austrian songwriter, Composer of operettas & film music	Composers , Musicians	San Marino	994
Story of Joseph		1100BC	Joseph's Coat of Many Colors - 24 Stamps	Special Issues	Guyana (24)	2834 Sheet
Story of Ruth & Naomi		1100BC	Biblical Story With Stamps - 24 stamps	Special Issues	Guyana (24)	1994 Sheet
Strauss	Johann	1825-1899	Austrian Waltz Composer	Composers , Musicians	Austria	560
Strauss	Johann	1825-1899	Austrian Waltz Composer	Composers , Musicians	Austria	1024

LAST NAME	FIRST NAME	DATES LIVED	FIELD OF KNOWLEDGE	HERO CLASSIFICATION	COUNTRY OF STAMP	SCOTT # OF STAMP
Strauss	Richard	1864-1949	Composer	Composers , Musicians	Austria	2507
Strauss	Johann	1825-1899	Austrian Waltz Composer	Composers , Musicians	Deutchland Germany	2045
Strauss	Sigmund	1869-1920	Businessman	Financiers, Businessmen	Austria	1024
Strauss	Johann	1825-1899	Vienese Composer of Operas	Composers , Musicians	Austria	873
Strauss II	Oscar	1870-1954	Vienese Composer of Operas	Composers , Musicians	Austria	872
Strauss II	Johann	1825-1899	Austrian Waltz Composer	Composers , Musicians	Monaco	997
Strauss II	Johann	1825-1899	Austrian Waltz Composer	Composers , Musicians	Monaco	998
Streisand	Barbara	1942-date	American Singer, Actress, Director	Actors, Entertainers	St. Vincent (9)	2011 Sheet
Sulzer	Solomon	1804-1890	Austrian Composer, Chazzan	Composers , Musicians	Austria	1488
Sverdlov	Jacob	1885-1919	1st. President of Russia after Revolution	National Government Leaders	Russia	5332
Sverdlovsk			City in Russia	Other	Russia	4131
Symbol With Crying Eye		1937-1945	Symbol	Other	St. Thomas & Prince Islands	2245 Sheet
Synagogue & Star of David		1937-1945	Symbol	Other	Romania	5417
Szabo	Ervin	1877-1929	Social Scientist, Hungary,Converted, born Samuel Schlesinger	Scientists	Hungary	2505
Szell	George	1897-1970	Hungarian-American Conductor of Orchestra	Musicians	United States	3160
Szenes	Hannah	1921-1944	Anti Nazi Paratrcpoper, Poet	Martyrs	Israel	831B
Szilard	Leo	1898-1964	German-Hungarian Nuclear Physicist	Scientists	Israel	3592
Szold	Henrietta	1860-1945	Founder of Hadassah Womens Org., Zionist	Zionists	Israel	188
Szoletesenek	Madach I.	1870-1970	Poet, Dramatist Writer	Writers	Hungary	2022
Tagger	Sionah	1892-1979	Painter, Artist - "Landscapes"	Artists, Painters	Israel	816
Tal	Mikhail	1936-1992	Soviet-Latvia Chess Master	Chess Masters	Cambodia	1554
Talmon	Jacob	1916-1980	Historian Writer	Writers	Israel	1554
Tamm	Igor	1895-1944	Nobel Prize for Physics	Scientists	St. Vincent	2220k
Tandler	Julius	1869-1936	Austrian Physician, Politician	Politicians	Austria	1358
Tauber (Taeuber)	Susanna(Sophie)	1889-1943	Swiss Artist, Painter, Sculptor, Dada Art Movement, Textile designs	Artists, Painters	Switzerland	2425
Tauber (Taeuber)	Susanna(Sophie)	1889-1943	Swss Artist, Painter, Sculptor, Dada Art Movement, Textile designs	Artists, Painters	Switzerland	2426
Taylor	Elizabeth	1932-2011	British American Actress	Actors, Entertainers	Mali	694
Tchernichovsky	Shaul	1875-1943	Poet	Writers	Israel	1269k
Tchernichovsky	Saul	1875-1943	Russian Hebrew Writer, Zionist	Zionists	Israel	1269k
Three Stooges	Larry, Curly, Moe		Comedy Film Actors - 1999 sheets	Actors, Entertainers	Senegal (2)	1433-34 M/S
Three Stooges	Larry, Curly, Moe		Comedy Film Actors - 1999 sheet	Actors, Entertainers	Senegal (9)	Sheet
Ticho	Anna	1894-1980	Artist of Jerusalem Hills	Artists, Painters	Israel	771
Tiomkin	Dimitri	1894-1975	Musician	Musicians	United States	3340
Torah			The Torah	Special Issues	Venezuela	159f
Toscanini	Arturo	1867-1957	Italian Musician & Conductor	Musicians	Israel (2)	955
Toscanini	Arturo	1867-1957	Italian Musician & Conductor	Musicians	Italy	2785
Touro Synagogue		1763-present	Oldest existing Synagogue in US, Newport, R.I	Other	United States	2017
Trotsky	Leon	1879-1940	born Lev Davidovich Bronstein Ukranian - Marxist, Revolutionary-baby stamp	Military	Russia	B49
Trumpeldor	Joseph	1880-1920	Military Hero, Zionist	Military	Israel	401
Trumpeldor	Joseph	1880-1920	Military Hero, Zionist	Military	Israel	741
Tucholsky	Kurt	1890-1935	Physician	Scientists	Hungary	1498
Tucholsky	Kurt	1890-1935	German Journalist, Satirist, Writer	Writers	Germany	9N506
Tucker	Richard	1913-1975	American Singer, Operetic	Musicians	United States	3155
Tuwim	Julian	1894-1953	Lyricist, Poet, Polish- Pseudonym, "Olden"	Writers	Poland	1714
Ussishkin	Menachem	1863-1941	Head of Jewish National Fund	Zionists	Israel	712
Usyskin	I.D.	1910-1934	Physicist, Russian, died in hot air balloon	Scientists	Russia	Mi480A
Vambery	Armenius (Armin)	1832-1913	Hungarian Turkologist & Traveller, Scientist	Writers	Russia	1104
Veil	Simone Annie	1927-2017	President of European Parliament, French Lawyer	Politicians	France	1650
Vogel	Sir Julius	1835-1899	Eighth Premier of New Zealand	National Government Leaders	New Zealand	678
Volodarsky (Goldshteyn)	Moisey (Markovich)	1891-1918	Russian Early Soviet Politician & Revolutionary	Politicians	Russia	516
Volynov	Boris	1934-date	Soviet Space Astronaut	Astronaut	Russia	3571 S/S
Von Lieben	Robert	1878-1913	Austrian Physicist	Scientists	Austria	B150
von Wilczek	Georgina		Wife of Franz Joseph 2nd, her great ucle was Franz Joseph 1st.	National Government Leaders	Lichtlenstein	186
Vysotsky	Vladimir Semyonovich	1938-1980	Russian singer, scngwriter, poet	Composers , Musicians	Armenia	1056
Weksman	Selman	1888-1973	Ukranian - American Inventor	Scientists	Gambia	910
Wallach	Otto	1847-1931	German Chemist-Nobel Prize in 1910	Scientists	Malagasy	1132k
Wallach	Otto	1847-1931	German Chemist-Nobel Prize in 1910	Scientists	Malagasy	1132k
Wallenberg	Raoul	1912-1947	Swedish Businessman,Diplomat	Financier, Businessman	Argentina	2026
Wallenberg	Raoul	1912-1947	Swedish Businessman,Diplomat _	Financier, Businessman	Dominica	1134
Wallenberg	Raoul	1912-1947	Swedish Businessman,Diplomat	Financier, Businessman	Israel	842
Wallenberg	Raoul	1912-1947	Swedish Businessman,Diplomat	Financier, Businessman	Sweden	1643
Wallenberg	Raoul	1912-1947	Swedish Businessman,Diplomat	Financier, Businessman	United States	3135
Wallenburg	Raoul	1912-1947	Swedish Diplomat- Saved many Jews in WW2	National Government Leaders	Hungary	4241
Warburg	Otto	1883-1970	German Physiologist, Botanist	Scientists	Germany	1400
Warski	Adolph	1868-1937	Polish Communist Movement Leader	Underground Heroes	Poland	2308

LAST NAME	FIRST NAME	DATES LIVED	FIELD OF KNOWLEDGE	HERO CLASSIFICATION	COUNTRY OF STAMP	SCOTT # OF STAMP
Waxman	Franz	1906-1967	German Musician, Conductor, Film Composer	Musicians	United States	3342
Weill	Kurt	1900-1950	German Composer	Composers , Musicians	Grenada Grenadines	1119 S/S
Weisenthal	Simone	1908-2005	Austrian Hunter of Nazi War Criminals	Financiers, Businessmen	Israel	1820
Weiser	Grethe	1903-1970	Married Jewish man- Financed Husband- Actress	Actors, Entertainers	Germany	1726
Weiss	Akiva Aryeh	1868-1947	Developer, Builder	Financiers, Businessmen	Israel	1717
Weiss	Yaavov	1924-1947	Martyr For Independence	Martyrs	Israel	831M
Weizmam	Chaim	1874-1952	First President of Israel	National Government Leaders	Israel	71
Weizman	Ezir	1924-2005	Government	National Government Leaders	Israel	1632
Weizmann	Chaim	1874-1952	First President of Israel	National Government Leaders	Israel	70
Weizmann	Chaim	1874-1952	First President of Israel	National Government Leaders	Israel	353
Weizmann	Chaim	1874-1952	First President of Israel	National Government Leaders	Israel	354
Weizmann	Chaim	1874-1952	First President of Israel	National Government Leaders	Israel	696
Weizmann	Chaim	1874-1952	1st President of Israel	National Government Leaders	St. Thomas & Prince Islands	2140 Sheet
Werfel	Franz	1890-1945	Czech Writer	Writers	Austria	1516
Werfel	Franz	1890-1945	Czech Writer	Writers	Deutchland Germany	1904
Wiener	Norbert	1894-1964	Swedish-American Mathematician, Cybernetics	Scientists	Israel	1133d
Wiener	Norbert	1894-1964	Mathmatic Studies	Scientists	Israel	1362d
Wiener	Alexander S.	1907-1976	New York leader in forensic medicine, discovered Rh blood factor	Scientists	United States (ENV)	1425
Wiensauski	Henry	1835-1880	Polish Violinist and Composer	Composers , Musicians	Poland	795
Wiensauski	Henry	1835-1880	Polish Violinist and Composer	Composers , Musicians	Poland	2482
Wiesel	Ellie	1928-date	Romanian Writer, Professor, Political Activist	Writers	Antigua	1947
Wilder	Billy	1906-2002	Austrian born Samuel Wilder, Actor, Producer, Filmmaker	Actors, Entertainers	United States	4670
Wilensky	Moshe	1910-1997	Polish Musician, Theatre Pianist	Musicians	Israel	1773H
Willson	Meredith	1902-1984	American Songwriter, Playwrite, Composer	Composers , Musicians	United States	3349
Willstatter	Richard	1872-1942	German Organic Chemist	Scientists	Sweden	1150
Wingate	General Charles O.	1903-1944	Military	Military	Israel	881
Wolffson	David	1856-1914	Banker	Financier, Businessman	Israel	888
Wynn (Leopold)	Ed (Isiah Edwin)	1886-1966	Actor, Comedian, Radio Show Host	Actors, Entertainers	Grenada Grenadines	1842
Yakir	Yona	1897-1937	General of Red Army, Victim of Stalin	Military	Russia	3187
Yalow	Roslyn	1921-2011	American Medical Physicist-1977 Nobel	Scientists	Sierre Leone	1844e
Zacuto	Abraham	1452-15`5	Rabbi	Rabbis	Sierre Leone	910
Zadkine	Ossip	1890-1967	Russian Artist, Sculptor, Painter, Lithos	Artists, Painters	France	2192
Zalman	Rabbi Solomon Elijah ben	1720-1797	Rabbi	Rabbis	Israel	1304
Zalman	Elijah ben Solomon	1720-1797	Rabbi	Rabbis	Israel	1904
Zalman	Elijah ben Solomon	1720-1797	Rabbi	Rabbis	Israel	1904
Zamenhoff	L.L.	1859-1917	Polish Language Inventor of Esperanto Language	Inventors	Germany	2617 M/S
Zamenhoff	L.L.	1859-1917	Polish language inventor of Esperanto Language	Inventors	Hungary	C170
Zaminhoff	L.L.	1859-1917	Polish Language Inventor of Esperanto Language	Inventors	Bulgaria	3231
Zaminhoff	L.L.	1859-1917	Polish Language Inventor of Esperanto Language	Inventors	Poland	859
Zaritsky	Joseph	1891-1985	Artist, Painter - "Jerusalem Painting"	Artists, Painters	Israel	772
Ze'evy	Rechavem	1926-2001	Minister of Israel	National Government Leaders	Israel	1484
Zetkin	Klara	1857-1933	Women's Rights Activist	Human Rights	Hungary	676
Zetkin (Eisner)	Klara (Clara)	1857-1933	German Marxist Activist for Women's Rights	Politicians	Hungary	1307
Zinneman	Fred	1907-1997	Austrian born Film Director,4 Academy Awards	Film	Austria	2203
Zola	Emile	1840-1902	French novelist, playwright	Writers	Czechoslovakia	2774
Zuckerman	Yitzhak	1915-1981	Resistance Hero	Underground Heroes	Israel	906
Zuckmeyer	Carl	1896-1977	German writer, Playwright	Writers	Germany	1950
Zvi	Izhak Ben	1884-1963	Zionist leader, Israel Historian	Zionists	Israel	255
Zweig	Arnold	1887-1968	German Soldier & Writer	Military	German Demokratic Republic	1941
Zweig	Arnold	1887-1968	German Soldier & Writer	Military	German Demokratic Republic	2604
Zweig	Arnold	1887-1968	German Soldier & Writer	Military	German Demokratic Republic	2604
Zweig	Stefan	1881-1942	Austrian Novelist, Playwrite	Writers	Austria	1199